From Albania, With Love

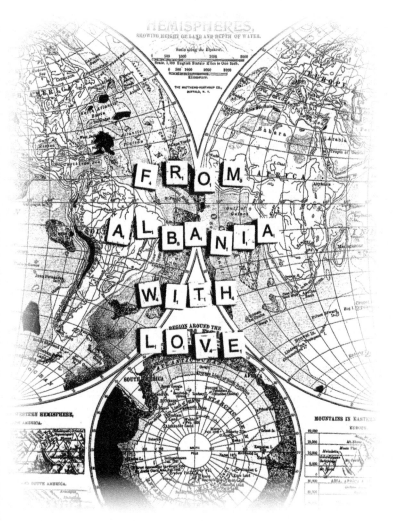

To Mom,

No galaxy in this universe could ever be big
enough to hold my love for you.

This memoir is my story. A story my soul was begging me to tell the world, but I often found myself waiting for the right time, for someone else to make it happen, and especially for a sign that this is what I was meant to do.

If you are looking for a sign to follow your dreams, this is it.

Go and live your dreams out loud, not just in your what ifs, your expectations, and the illusion of perfect timing.

With Love,
Migena

From Albania, With Love

A collection of true stories.

CONTENT

Fair Warning:

I like to think of myself as an honest girl, so keeping that in mind, here are two very fair warnings before you read any further.

1. There will be swearing (probably a lot). Honesty, remember?

2. You might not like my honesty or opinions. Shocker, I know, but sensitivity seems to run high these days. If you don't like my opinions or me, get in line – it probably wraps around the block.

From Albania, With Love

PRELUDE
A Semi Scientific Experiment

You know that weirdly freeing feeling of walking around your house naked without giving a shit if anybody can see you? Or – maybe this is better – finally telling that one person that you hate that they do in fact suck, that's the feeling surging through my veins right now. Pure freedom, much like pure ecstasy or cocaine and no, I have never done either of those things.

I have a scar on my forehead – not like Harry Potter – you can barely see mine. It's on the middle left side and it's basically invisible unless you run your fingers over it. Why is this relevant? Stay with me. I promise there is a point.

I was around four or five – I can't really remember, when I got the scar. My sister was always the popular one, the more social one, the better liked, and no I am not looking for anybody's sympathy – I am just peachy. My point is that she had lots of friends when we were younger and I was the tag along.

You know, the younger sibling that your mom makes you take when you hang out with your friends, but you really never want to. One day, my sister refused or didn't wait for me. I am not sure which it was and it doesn't really matter.

Now, if you couldn't tell from my name – I am in fact not from the great United States of America, but from

Albania (I will get to that later and I know you are pulling up Google to see where that is). Much of the neighborhood where my parents lived was made up of concrete apartment buildings and some shotty construction work so there were no pretty streets, colorful flowers, white picket fences or overly precautious and sensitive parents around.

When my mom told me that my sister had left or was just about to leave with her friends – I hurried to wear my rubber flat sandals and chase after her, not wanting to be left out.

That last part, about not wanting to be left out – remember it, because it's the whole point of this pure, honest, and no fucks given book.

Too soon with the swearing? Oh well!

As I ran down three flights of concrete stairs, my eyes caught my sister leaving with her friends, so I booked it. Bad idea.

I did not arrive to the bottom of the stairs – my head arrived. You guessed it, I tripped and my head went flying forward. Remember the shotty construction? Well, a very durable and thin piece of metal was sticking out at the bottom of the concrete stairs. I did not die, obviously, but I am pretty sure I blacked out and my sister felt terrible – as she should have.

That's the scar I was talking about, the one on my forehead – which I notice almost every day when I am doing my makeup or washing my face. It should have been my constant reminder that trying to fit in is dangerous for your health, but I was young and stupid so forward I trotted, until we arrived to this point.

Me, typing these words at 9:30PM and so very far from the child who tripped and split her head open just to fit in and have people like her.

How did we get here you ask? That, my friends, is the point of this long overdue story. Another good question you are probably asking yourself is why in the fuck should you care? You shouldn't. In fact, you don't have to – that's the beauty of life, time, and the US of A.

Freedom.

You don't like it, you walk away. You don't like me or my foul mouth, you close the book.

Hell, I don't even know if I am ever going to send this out to be published/represented.

However, if you still care and want me to answer that question, here is the simple truth.

I am 25 years old. I was born in Fier, Albania. I live in Massachusetts right now even though the west coast is looking really good. Most importantly: for the past two years, I have actively been querying literary agents in an attempt to get my novel published.

Why should this be the answer to your question of giving a shit about me or what I am now writing?

Because, my journey has not ended, because the publishing world is heart breaking and soul wrenching, because I am really tired, because I am sick of constantly guarding myself/what I say, because I don't want to fit in anymore, because my background is not a trend for twitter, movies, or books, because I just want to be honest.

I know what you are thinking – get a blog loser! I have one, so save it. My blog is about my publishing journey and I am mostly using it as a vantage point for when I hopefully "make it", but mostly it's just a helpful guide for people who are also getting into writing and the scary publishing world.

Truthfully, I was hoping on recording my struggles with hope of one day breaking through and people then being inspired by my journey. Well, there has been plenty of struggle, but no happy ending. Yet.

Let's get back on track.

This will probably be the most honest piece I will ever write and no – I don't mean that I will be dishonest on other work, but I was put on this earth to write fiction, using my imagination, and I have. Most of it is very heavily based on my own experiences, without basically saying the characters are me, but this is me.

This story, a 25-year-old immigrant, from a country most people can't point out on a map, is my story. A story of coming of age, a story of first crushes, a story of lessons, a story of friendship, a story of first love, a story of finding where you belong, a story of mistakes, a story of trying to find out who you want to become, and most importantly to me, a story of trying to get a message to the world in hopes of leaving it a tad better than I found it.

From Albania, With Love

Don't get caught up though – while I am very romantic (as romantic as someone can get when they love reading Shakespearean tragedies and Dante's Inferno) I don't know if this story will have a happy ending. We will get there together…sort of like a weird, unfiltered diary of the past and present, and you have a front row view.

So, why would I do this?

I have a theory.

I am in the middle of revising my second book (I am writing a series – we will get to that, I promise). I find myself frustrated most days and I bitch to my sister, a lot. It's excessive, but there is a reason behind it, which we will also get to.

My theory?

What would happen if I sit down and write nothing but the truth? I know it's actually a question, but just stay with me. Time will not end. The world will not stop spinning. People will still continue to be annoying. And just maybe, I will feel a bit freer. The truth sets you free, right?

So, I am taking a break (this is a HUGE deal, by the way – you'll see why). It's not much of a break as I will continue to write, but still, a break from my made-up worlds.

Today is Thursday. I am giving myself until Monday at midnight – a sort of warped college reality in which you have until midnight to complete the assignment – to complete this story of me in hope that things will be calmer, more organized and I will feel like myself again or who I want to become.

At the end, I will decide if I want to submit this to be published, if it will even draw an interest. For now, it will just be me, unfiltered, authentic, and not thinking about anything else but my story.

I know what you're thinking – holy shit! What about all the people in your life you are going to talk about? I'm not stupid, just so we are clear and yes, that reason has been a main factor as to why I haven't done this before, however, remember I said this is just for me? It is. Just in case I do decide to share this with the world and to save myself hours of editing (editing sucks sometimes) this will be an "allegedly" type of story.

What do I mean?

You know when you watch gossip news, or read those trashy magazines at the check-out counter and they say Selena Gomez is allegedly dating the Weeknd, or Ed Sheeran's new single is allegedly about a recent famous ex. They don't say it because they don't know – they say it because they don't want to get sued.

These various stories you are going to read about the various topics I mentioned will feature very real people with very fake names, because allegedly.

Allegedly, this is the real-life story of Migena Dulaj – a 25-year-old, immigrant with a handful of stories she wants to share. In honesty, this is the story of any 25-year-old immigrant, trying to get published, that also has a handful of stories and lessons she wants to share with the world.

From Albania, With Love

Just like I am not stupid, I am also not frightened easily so don't think I am giving people fake names because I am scared. I just don't want to give them attention.

Why?

Because most of them don't fucking deserve any sort of light shed on them, and this is my story, not theirs. If they want their story told, they can shed a few tears and attempt to write a book. I will not lie to make myself sound better or tarnish someone's reputation, because honesty – remember?

So, where are we? What even is this?

It's a super long prelude, but simple – it's a story book of a little girl that wanted to fit in, until she realized she had a much bigger message for all the little girls out there with weird names or not, from a known country or not, with small or big dreams.

Anything is possible and I know, I said we don't know if this is a happy ending, but finding out who you want to be is a long, long journey and I guarantee, it's almost never about how it all ends because nobody cares when the story ends.

Do you think people want to hear the end of Romeo & Juliet or how they fell in love? I know – it's not the best example, but you get it.

How will this be structured?

What the fuck? Who cares?

I care.

I love structure and organization, remember that – very important for later.

For my fellow neat freaks out there, I don't know how this will be planned as I am just writing without really thinking about it. Freedom. But, once a neat freak, always a neat freak and if I don't have a loose plan, I will just continue writing forever. I was that kid in school that could fill the word or page requirement for an assignment faster than anybody and always asked for extra paper on the written part of the test, so I am thinking at the end of each chapter, there will be a lesson of the day or lesson of the chapter.

Yeah – I like that. Lesson of the chapter.

Look at you! 2,000 words and you are still here.

The real stories begin now so buckle up kids because this will be a long ass, truthful and sometimes painful journey.

I will see you on the other side – closer to the back cover.

CHAPTER 1
Republic of Albania

Alright, boys and girls – we are off. I meant to start writing when I actually got up at 8AM this morning, but I live in the frustratingly snow covered east coast. I had to clean my car and rev it over the snow to go to Starbucks and get coffee. I know – white people problems, but I am addicted and I needed all my energy for today's writing session. Looking into the past is exhausting.

With two Trenta iced coffees, (I don't like hot coffee) I am all set to start this journey/honest diary for the next three days.

Since these life lessons will be from my point of view and a lot about me, I thought you should know about Albania – remember, I was born there and it's the main reason why my life went the way it did. I am giving you a break from me, or you can think of it as background information before the real story is presented. Sort of like when you watch a movie and they introduce you to distant family members for no apparent reason, but it's actually so you can think the main character is the best or honorable – you take your pick.

Also, please don't skip over this chapter. It will be like not laying down a foundation when you build a house. You will see all the interesting sections of the house, but then it will fall and you'll be pissed. In this case, you'll spent two hours reading something that makes no sense in the end.

I know history is not most people's favorite subject in school, but I promise, it will be painless and maybe a little interesting.

If you pulled up a map, you know by now that Albania is surrounded by Macedonia, Montenegro, and Kosovo.

Still don't know where I am talking about?

Here's a better explanation – it's above Greece and across Italy's heel. I can hear most of you saying, "Ohhh, okay."

Also, I know the very little facts you know about my home country are actually not accurate. How do I know? Media is a liar.

You probably think Albania is made up of criminals because Taken 1, Taken 2, Taken 3 and so on. You think I'm being a pessimist? In Harry Potter, Lord Voldemort – the evilest, most un-liked character in children's fiction hid in Albania, at one point in the series.

Also, you probably think that all Albanian girls fear their daddy, like to play house, magically go to the best colleges, and then they suddenly turn to hoes because they have been restrained their whole life. Or maybe, you think we were all filtered through sex trading, because there is another "fact" people think they know about Albania.

Oh, and how could I forget about the mafia. You know that one friend that you maybe have who is Albanian that tells you her family is in the mafia just to impress you? They aren't. I am definitely not saying the Albanian mafia doesn't exist, but I am just saying that you would not know they were part of it – Trust me.

Underrepresented cultures in America?

Try nonexistent. We don't have neighborhoods. We don't have a corner stores. We don't have large parades. We rarely, rarely have restaurants. Schools group us in Eastern Europe when having any sort of culture day.

Why does this unjust stereo typing happen?

Lack of knowledge and it's nobody's fault in particular, but I'm here to right all the wrongs.

Let's get to the history and a few true facts.

Albania has been around for a long, long time – like 4th Century BC, type of long time. It was technically part of Illyria back in the day, but I will not go that far as it is not necessary. After that time period, there were the middle ages, then there was the Ottoman Empire. They started taking Albania in 1415 and by 1431 they occupied most of Albania. An important fact to remember here is that Albania was heavily Catholic and Orthodox before the Ottoman Empire strutted into our lands and introduced Islam. Three religions in one small country.

Fun fact: my dad is Muslim and my mom is Orthodox.

We will get to that later.

From all this ancient history, the most important fact or man is Gjergj Kastrioti Skënderbeu. He was and *still* is a national hero and let me remind you, we are talking about 574 years ago. So, what did he do that was sooo great?

Gjergj Kastrioti Skënderbeu was born on May 6th, 1405 and he was an Albanian nobleman and military commander who served in the Ottoman Empire from 1423 until 1443. A member of the noble Kastrioti family, he was sent as a hostage to the Ottoman court much like the horse in Troy. He was educated and entered the service of the Ottoman sultan for 20 years. He quietly rose through the ranks and became a sanjakbey (governor) in 1440.

Can you imagine?

We can't even do a group project with people we don't like and this man spent 20 years with these people he was trying to take down. National hero.

Anyway, so to the Battle of Nish we arrive. It was actually five different battles; first they took the town of Nish, then three battles against Ottoman armies advancing towards Nish, then finally, one last battle against the remaining three Ottoman Empire armies. Who were these people attacking the Ottoman city of Nish?

Christian contingents.

Religious wars have been around for decades and decades, so we won't spend too much time on this. Back to our national hero.

Skënderbeu was at that battle and that's when he rose to his purpose – what he had been waiting for. He deserted the Ottoman army at the Battle of Nish, along with his nephew, Hamza Kastrioti, and 300 loyal Albanians. They captured Kruje, a city which now stands just outside of Albania's capital, and then his real work began – a 25-year long struggle against the Ottoman Empire.

For 25 years, Skënderbeu defended Kruje and the castle it stood upon along with the Albanian people. He built his army up to 10,000 men, and with their support he took back many lands which were Albanian before they were swallowed into the Ottoman Empire.

His military skills and the undying support he had from his soldiers allowed him to defeat larger Ottoman armies and also halted the expansion of the Empire many times. He was revered and considered a model Christian resistance against the Ottoman Muslims.

Now, I know what you're thinking. It sounds like I am taking the Christian side and I'm not – religion has always been a weird subject for me, but we will get to that later.

Gjergj Kastrioti Skënderbeu was factually remembered as a model Christian in history books, but to the people, the people I have known and continue to know in Albania, it was not about faith. It was about hope, resistance, identity, and an overall sense of freedom on their land. He was the first symbol they had of standing up for yourself, defending your country and your people, and doing the right thing no matter how long it takes.

The reason why I spent almost two pages talking about him is because nobody really knows where he was in fact born. There are many theories, but lands were so overlapping, armies over one another, empires constantly expanding that there is no specific location, and that is the whole point. That's what he showed the people. He showed them humanity. He showed them what brothers and sisters in arms can do. He showed them what unity instead of division looked like.

Just people fighting for something they believed in.

And, he was as humble as they come.

"I have not brought you liberty, I found it here, among you."

I mean, come on.

Now, you are probably wondering why Albania did not go on to conquer the world like the British Empire. They did have the most fearless and badass general on their side.

Remember when I told you that nobody wants the end of a story? Well, I think people would take the end over what happens after, any day. You would much rather hear the story of Cinderella and the Prince getting married, than, the story of Cinderella getting fed up with her perfect Prince after the wedding because if we are being honest – he was just a jackass, finding love with a damn lost shoe.

Happily ever after is just a story that has not ended.

So, when our national hero died, the Ottoman Empire continued, because you guessed it, they had the power of a fucking Empire. Albania remained under the Ottoman Empire until 1912 as part of Rumelia. In the meantime, most of the citizens converted to Islam and contribute to current day statistics reading 56.7% of all Albanians practice Islam – but there's a catch.

From Albania, With Love

What happened in 1912?

Without going into too much detail, another national hero is Ismail Qemali, who proclaimed independence for Albania after the Balkan Wars. Now that I think about it – it sort of sucked to be him. I mean, yes, everybody remembers independence, but more people remember Gjergj Kastrioti Skënderbeu. I guess, it's hard to forget someone who sacrifices 45 years fighting for the people.

Anyway, November 28th, 1912, Albania was independent and free! Time to relish in the history and party on the streets. Right?

Wrong.

Anybody who has ever done anything will tell you that the beginning is the hardest part and I know, technically this is not the beginning beginning, but decades of history, religion, oppression, and anything else you can think of, does not necessarily help in strengthening a young country.

There is a lot of in between history from this point to the one we are getting too, and I promised not to be boring so here is an over view:

1912 – Independence

1913 – Independence recognized at the Conference of London (official recognition or it didn't happen.)

1914 – 1925 – Principality

1925 – 1928 – Albanian Republic

1928 – Monarchy (I know…what the fuck were we thinking?)

1939 – 1944 – Albanian Kingdom

1939 – Conquered by Italy (Mussolini and his beady eyes)

1941 – The rise of Enver Hoxha

1943 – Conquered by Nazi Germany

1944 – Communism

1985 – The fall of Enver Hoxha

1992 – Democracy

You know those heavy, bulky books you put around your apartment or house to make it seem like you are a scholar and actually like to read about world history - the ones with dictators usually featuring Hitler, Stalin and Mussolini on the front cover? When you open the book, and go to the Eastern European section, even though Albania is not in Eastern Europe, there you will find Enver Hoxha.

Look up at that list of dates I gave you.

1941 - Enver Hoxha.

I literally just took a deep breath because I don't even know where to begin – actually, I do...I just...ugh. Okay, from the top.

Albania was passed around like a terrible game of hot potato during World War II. Italy then Germany – Russia dabbled in a bit too, until 1941 when a small Albanian Communist group established in our capital of Tirana. The 130 members were led by no other than Enver Hoxha. By the end of WWII, they had armies – loyal and blinded men who, in 1945, were sent to northern Albania to eliminate rivals. These rivals were the Kelmendi people, but they stood no chance against Hoxha's ride or die soldiers. The Kelmendi were killed or tortured. Then – oh did you think it ended there?

Then, class struggle was applied; human freedoms and human rights were denied *AND* the Kelmend region was isolated by both border and lack of accessible roads for 20 years.

20 fucking years.

The introduction to Enver Hoxha, ladies and gentlemen.

Yes, you read that right – introduction, because he ruled over Albania until 1985.

This is the story after happily ever after.

Okay, I know – you are probably thinking: Damn! She said this would be quick and she is just starting the story?

The reason why I am saying this is the start of the story is because I remember this the best, and it has the most influence on my life. My parents lived under Enver Hoxha's rule and without making this long, here are a few things he did:

- ♦ Forced atheism.
- ♦ Enforced inhumane torture tactics.
- ♦ Formed the secret police.
- ♦ Built concentration prisons.
- ♦ Banned divorce.
- ♦ Created extreme nationalism.
- ♦ Banned beards to enforce atheism in a previously Muslim popular country.

♦ Built a wall around the borders which would electrocute people.

♦ Ordered instant death (without trial) for conspirators against his rule.

So, that was my parents Albania, my grandparents Albania and most of my family's Albania. While this may come as a shock to you, not everybody was opposed to him – he increased the economy and everybody was taken care of (employment, nutrition, and financial). The ones who didn't like him, did not dare say anything. The secret police you see on that list, up top – they reported if anybody spoke ill of the leader and you know what happened?

I can tell you one thing, freedom of speech was not accepted.

You spoke ill of Enver Hoxha or the government – they introduced you to the firing squad. Without trial, by the way.

Why am I telling you this?

Are my fellow Albanians angry that I painted such an ugly picture?

I don't give a shit, because this is my story. The foundation that I mentioned is this. Knowing how my parents were raised, knowing that the country I was born in declared democracy the same year I was born, knowing the vast difference between there and here, knowing why I will take actions which I will realize are mistakes, knowing my behavior and choices over the rest of these stories, and especially knowing how difficult it is for someone raised in such an environment to make free choices that determine who you are.

What happened after Hoxha?

You can look it up. I told you this was a history lesson – not current affairs.

If you are really interested; we stand at a parliamentary republic system as a country, and the two major political parties are the socialist party and the democratic party.

The rest is as you can imagine it – cutthroat politics, parties constantly fighting, and dirty politicians.

So, kids, that's it! You made it...hopefully. Now you can tell someone a real fun fact about Albania and then spend 15 minutes explaining to that person where Albania is on a map.

Oh, I almost forgot....

Lesson of the Chapter:

Oppression is a chance to discover what is truly important.

CHAPTER 2

I Was Born A Boy

I know what you're thinking.

Dear God. She's hitting us with the hard stuff right off the bat, especially after the history lesson.

Calm down. I am a girl, and I have always been a girl – trust me. Maybe I did not start this where I should have. Remember Hoxha?

Why am I even asking – of course you do.

Well, as you can probably guess, he was not a fan of women. Or, I should say – women's rights, women being anything but someone's wife, women working, and God forbid women being equal to men.

Why does this matter?

His ideals led to a traditional country. Divorce was against the law and having a boy born into the family was basically normal or required. After Hoxha, life moved on; people got married, had kids, went to work and so on. You get the idea, but some ideals are hard to break especially if the same psychopath ruled for 44 years.

To me, it is archaic. Wanting a boy in the family because only he can carry the family name and honor like we are some sort of French Noble family circa 1512. It's bullshit. Call me a raging feminist, call me a woman, call me whatever you want, because, you guessed it, I don't give a shit.

Where were we?

Oh, yeah…back to my family.

I have a very, very large family. The type of large in which when you meet more family members you just call them uncle or cousin because they probably are just that, somewhere down the family tree. My father has four sisters and one brother; my mom has two sisters and one brother. Mostly all are married, but let's focus on my dad's side. You'll see why.

All my father's siblings are married and have kids. They all had one boy and one girl. I know… something was definitely in the water, and no I am not joking. My dad is the oldest then come his four sisters then comes his young brother. All his sisters had one son and one daughter and everybody stopped at two kids. His young brother had two boys.

So, my sister was born, four years ahead of me.

Everybody was so excited – the eldest of the family just had his first baby. The honor, the love, the pride…. The stone age or so it felt like it to me.

You might think I'm being bitter, so I will just come out and say this now. I love my sister, so this story has nothing to do with how much my family adored her and still does – she's a people person type of girl.

Four years passed and my family waited…not so patiently, for the boy of the family to be born, and keep in mind two kids was the norm.

If you ask anybody in my family, they will tell you they basically all made their mind up that I was going to be a

21

boy. If you ask me, they were all crazy and some still are. Not because I obviously know I'm a girl, but because my mom never found out what the sex was – I don't think that sort of technology was available in 1992 Albania.

The time came for me to be born, and everybody was at the hospital, but my mom refused. She's a very hardheaded woman and I am proud to say I take after her.

Why in the world would she refuse to give birth?

The date. It was February 29th, 1992, and there was no way my mom was going to have a leap year baby. Her baby would not be five years old when she was actually 20 years old. So, she held off as long as she could, and apparently, I heard her loud and clear.

I was born on March 1st, 1992. A healthy baby girl.

Why do guys think some girls become strippers? Why do guys think some girls freak out on them sometimes? Why do guys think that some girls sleep around? Why do guys think some girls are insecure?

Daddy issues.

I know – extremely weird way to connect this story, but just stay with me.

When I was born, most of my family was extremely disappointed since I was missing a certain body part which would make me what they wanted. My father was the most disappointed and I know what you men out there are thinking.

Well, okay – he is allowed some disappointment. He wanted to have a son and teach him all the things he knew. The pride and joy of his life.

Yes, he was allowed a split second of disappointment and then he should have pulled it together, held his newborn baby girl, thanked his wife who just pushed a baby out of her vagina, and gotten the fuck over it. You can probably tell from my tone that none of those things happened.

He left.

Settle down. I don't mean left my mom or the family. He left the hospital and did not come back to pick us up. His younger brother came and picked my mom and I up from the hospital.

Welcome to daddy issues.

Population: Millions of girls everywhere, not including me.

Why?

I didn't find out he did that until recently, but there was plenty there to hint at the fact that he wanted a boy – desperately. Up until the age of eight, my father took me to the barber and gave me a bowl cut. No long hair for me, but my sister and I put tights on our head.

Don't look at me like that.

We wanted to know what long hair felt like – my mom had long hair so we would walk around the house and swing thin tights around pretending it was hair. We didn't know any better than to ask for what we wanted. It was not advisable for young girls to speak their mind or contradict their parents.

Then there is the fact that my father still calls me daddy's little boy – it's an endearing term, but still, I don't think boys would be okay with their mother calling them mommy's little girl, because she wanted a girl.

The bullshit women put up with, I swear.

Obviously, I don't hold it against my father and it's not like we have some broken, sad, daddy issues relationship, however it was the second step for me. Remember when I split my head open to fit in?

This was the second, unknowing thing I did to fit in and want to be loved. I played along and yes, I know I did not become a stripper as a result of my relationship with my father, but children are impressionable. They don't know what fear is, but subconsciously they fear not being loved and accepted – so they make up for it by looking around for examples of what people want them to act like, they internalize it, and then they act upon it.

I'm getting all Sigmund Freud on you, but trust me. A life time of internalizing does not end well and you'll see how catastrophically damaging it can be for the soul.

So why don't I have daddy issues?

Life and my grandparents (on my mom's side, let's be clear about that).

I know that's not a great explanation, but there is much more to the story, which we will get to in other chapters. This is just the beginning...see what I did there. If you don't – re read the last chapter.

From Albania, With Love

For all the men out there asking me, so then why do other girls have daddy issues?

There could be a multitude of different reasons, but to me there are two real reasons.

One: A father is the first man a girl falls in love with. Now, I promised to be honest so I will tell you I do love my father, I want the best for him, but he was not the first man I loved – that's another chapter.

Two: A father is the primary example of how men should treat a girl for the rest of her life. Remember the Albania my father was raised in – with Hoxha and the lasting effects of his poisonous rule on opinions and life styles. Some people are strong enough to make up their own mind and some fall into the social norm.

Does this sound vague to you?

Here's the deal; I became one of the people strong enough to make up my own mind, thanks to my father's opinions and words over the years. Positive or negative influence…?

You'll have to wait around and see.

For now, just know, sometimes, girls decide to listen to themselves and their own self-worth, and you would be lucky as hell to have one of those girls in your life.

Instead of asking me why do girls have daddy issues, maybe you should just treat girls right.

Oh, wow. There's an idea.

Lesson of the Chapter:

Sometimes, the people closest to us, hurt us the most.

CHAPTER 3

It's Okay, We're Friends

A	lcohol was never a prohibited item in my family. I mean – some stereotypes are true. For example; Albanians can handle their liquor, and we do drink a lot, but it's not vodka. It's raki. Raki is some strong shit man. I guess you can say it's sort of like gin with no brand.

What's that supposed to mean? It means, everybody in Albania makes it.

If you ever have the chance to go to an Albanians house, look for an unlabeled, plastic 2-liter bottle of Coke or Pepsi filled with clear liquid. It's raki. One whiff and you'll know.

My point?

Alcohol in college was not something new for me. Don't get me wrong – I didn't sit around when I was six and take shots to the head, but I did not have this raging desire to get wasted on my first weekend at college and then spend all of Sunday crying on the phone to my mom because I got transported.

I can still take shots like a champ, but nothing like when I was in college. 14 shots of vodka and I could walk a straight line, which made me the designated…no, not driver – you idiot. Don't ever do shit like that!

It made me the designated story keeper. If I was a champ at taking shots, I was the Michael Jordan of remembering what happened the night before. There is a fine line…actually a shot glass – you know if you take it, you're gone for the night and if you don't – you're just buzzed enough to have a great time and remember details. Most of my friends, freshman year, always forgot that fact, so Saturday morning at brunch I told them what they did the night before. If they left with a guy, if they threw up, if they got in someone's face, if they flashed someone. Honesty, remember?

As much as it became my talent later on in life, I was not too gifted when I was younger. Granted, a recent study found that a child doesn't remember much before the age of seven, so it's not my fault. My family reminds me of this story any chance they get, but I don't remember any detail of it. The only thing it reassures me of is the type of sister, friend, and person I am.

Before, I tell you this story I want you to know that I am really not crazy and I don't condone physical violence.

Remember my sister? Older than me, a people person, adored by the family and popular in the friend department. Here's a quick lesson – a people person personality also means quiet and appeasing. You know, those people that just say something so you don't fight, because maybe they don't like confrontation or maybe they are soft spoken. Now, I don't like confrontation, unless I truly care about the subject or person. I don't have a short fuse – not much gets me riled up.

The margin is very small, but there are a few things like bullies. I apparently didn't like them when I was younger and I still despise them.

Here is how the story goes;

My parents, my sister and myself were walking to my grandmother's house and we stopped at the local fabric shop – I know it sounds like something out of a once upon a time story, but we did walk most places and not much was premade; dresses, curtains, table cloths, etc. My mom still loves looking at fabric and I don't mind the trip to the store.

Back to the story. Just like my sister, my dad was very popular – he knew almost the whole damn city and we ran into a family he knew. If you have even gone shopping with your parents and they don't run into someone they know – consider yourself lucky. For the rest of us, we might as well take a nap and wait for the conversation to be over.

The couple my parents ran into had a daughter – their only daughter. As they began talking, we went outside; my sister, me and their daughter – let's call her Berta. I don't know why I picked that name.

We began playing and twirling and just running around like kids do. Now, as you will get to know me throughout these stories, let's begin with a fun fact.

I don't like pants. I don't like wearing them. I don't like how they look. I don't like how constricting they are. The list goes on, but I adore dresses and skirts. For being such a daddy's boy – I guess that was the most feminine thing about me. I especially love pleated skirts – super random, I know.

In Albania, skirts with pleats were very popular, so my mom always dressed us in them. On this particularly sunny day, all three of us were wearing pleated skirts – me, my sister, and Berta. So, as we twirled away and pointed out how our skirts were blowing in the wind, Berta decided to start some shit.

"Look!" my sister exclaimed. "My skirt twirls the most!"

"Yeah, well mine does too," Berta pouted, as she continued to twirl.

"No, but look," my sister smiled. "My skirt is better."

Ya'll this is so childish, but anyways.

"No," Berta stomped her foot. "Mine is better."

I don't know what I was doing at this point. How do I know this conversation happened? Because I just asked my mom to retell it for me.

After shouting about her skirt being better, Berta charged towards my sister and pushed her to the ground. My sister fell, but did not say anything.

Hell, to the no.

"Hey! She is going to kill this girl."

That's what my mom remembers hearing before all of them turned to see me on the ground over Berta with my hands comfortably wrapped around her neck.

Freeze frame.

From Albania, With Love

Let me remind you – I was three years old and my sister was seven. I am pretty sure Berta was somewhere around five or six, not that it matters. She was a bully and I was not about to let my sister be pushed around.

Remember that whole thing I told you about a child's fear and reflecting what they see around them?

My sister got pushed and didn't say anything, so my clue would have been to do the same, but instead I went full WWE on Berta.

Hint number three that I was never meant to fit in – I had a mind of my own and still do.

Berta's parents brushed it off as did my parents. They basically told her to walk it off. Serves her right.

Why am I telling the story of my aggressive delinquency as a child?

Most things, as I have talked about before, start from childhood without noticing it. I've always had a protective instinct since as long as I can remember. I am the type of person who goes all in or nothing. Sure, I have acquaintances and I am not one of those clingy girls that wants to hear I love yous after the fifth date – trust me, I need my damn space – but once I've decided your worth it, I'm all in.

110%, especially in friendships.

I bring this up now to set up the rest of my stories – little pieces of me at a time, remember? I guess you can also say, everything will always tie back to my attempt of fitting in. It will be like the hot button topic when you go to a therapist. The root of all evil.

It's an honorable characteristic to have – protective. You see it among leaders, soldiers, heroines in books, protagonists in movies, doctors, teachers, your mom, etc. It feels good to protect the people you love and I never thought much into it. I never protected the people I loved because I thought it would give me something in return, and I was never upset if they needed me at any time.

110%.

It was the reason why I didn't mind getting up at 1:35AM on Saturday night as a freshman in college to rescue my friend from some guy who wouldn't stop grinding up on her. This friend will probably come up again so let's name her Naira.

You think I was a badass when I took Berta down? This dude Naira was "dancing" with was a large football player, but I didn't give a shit. Maybe it was because I had just woken up cranky or maybe I don't have patience for people who can't catch a hint.

Back on track we go. I am trying my best to stay in chronological order. It will help in the end, but small stories will pop up here and there.

So, I am a protective heroine, but all heroines have flaws or maybe they just walk into problems without realizing it.

You want to know the problem with constantly protecting everybody around you, everybody you love?

You forget to protect yourself.

Lesson of the Chapter:

You can't protect those you love, if you don't protect yourself first.

CHAPTER 4

Rain Soaked Dirt

Albanians are simple. We like simple. Our town names have been around for decades, the whole country drives Benzes, our beaches are named after the town, no two words mean the same thing, our food is labeled for what it is, and on and on.

Here come the Debby downers:

Simple? What about the Albanian language having 36 letters, or the long names you give your kids, or the weird food you make?

Weird is a funny word. It's never used for a positive description, but almost always the item or food or experience a person might describe as weird is something they have never tried before. Why? Because most people fear the unknown.

Where was I?

Oh, yeah…simplicity. Where I am really trying to go with this is in the food department. When I moved to the States, I was so confused. As you can imagine the English language is very confusing. One word meaning two things? Try four or five different things. It does not seem weird to you US born, English was my first language people out there, but for a quick example let's take the word right – forget the spelling, just sound it out.

Write – Are you writing something down?

Right – Are you right in an argument?

Right – Are you making a right turn?

Right – Are you doing the right thing?

What. The. Fuck.

The English language or should I say America is perplexing and food descriptions and names are just as equally unclear. You all have these elaborate names for things and they don't come anywhere near describing what you are actually eating.

Bear claws.... This is actually a dessert, not a real bear hand.

Deviled eggs...No, you won't be possessed if you eat these eggs which are basically split in half and stuffed.

Pigs in a blanket.... Jesus Christ. Just call them little sausages wrapped in dough.

Cobb salad... Who the fuck is Cobb?

Cheesecake.... I just can't.

I did not try cheesecake until I was in college because the idea freaked me out. Why would I eat a cake made of cheese? Unappealing to me, until I realized that much like everything else in the English language, it means something completely different.

In Albania, our food might seem different to you, but we call it as we see it. I have a lot of different favorite Albanian dishes, but my favorite of all time is fasule. Fasule is a basic bean soup. Fasule are beans in Albanian.

See? It's not hard – just tell me what I'm eating!

Fasule is not the most radically different dish you will ever taste and it's nowhere near as delicious as some other things my mom makes, but it has a memory attached to it. It's sort of like how every damn American born person I have ever met who claims a peanut butter and jelly sandwich is the best thing they have ever had.

Here's a hint – it's not.

Not that I would know – I've never had one, but you remember childhood. That's why you like those sandwiches. They remind you of youth, of no fear, of a simpler time. It's a warm memory and that's what fasule is for me.

Up until the age of eight, I lived with my grandparents, on my mom's side.

Relax!

It was not because I was a girl and my family hated me – they aren't that fucked up. They have a whole other set of issues. I lived with my grandparents because it was easier for my mom. Walking distance, from my parents' apartment to my grandparents' house was about 40 minutes. My preschool was across the street from my grandparents' house, so it made no sense for my mom and I to get up at 5AM every morning, just so she could drop me off at school before going to work. Why didn't my dad get up at 5AM and help? I think you already know the answer to that, so I won't even bother.

When I say, across the street, I mean seven steps across the house. It was better for everybody and my sister remained with my parents as she was actually in elementary school so my mom helped her with homework and such.

From Albania, With Love

I know what this will sound like to you, but I promised to be honest. The time I spent living with my grandparents was the last time I truly remember happiness. That is what happy is supposed to feel like. No, I am not getting all heavy on you, but just remember this for later. I didn't know that I should have cataloged that feeling until it was too little too late.

What was it like? It was the best.

Fun fact: The climate in Albania, especially in Fier – where I lived – is incredible. A steady 60 to 70 degrees most of the year. From November till late February it would get a bit nippy, but at most, it would rain and I didn't mind it. I love rain, the smell of rain, the sound of rain – I'm even okay with thunder. I had never felt or touched snow until I moved to the States. A story for later.

My grandparents' house was beautiful. You took a tight left turn from the main street in town and in about 500 feet, you could see the exterior of the house, on the right. There was a gate around the house, but it was not iron and scary, and guarded like some sort of royal family. It was an ivy wall. There was no real brick wall anywhere in sight – just pure, lush green ivy from the outside and inside. It had created its own support, its own spine. Trust me – I would run into it when I was a kid. It was fun to hear the ivy rustle and move around, the soft, velvet like petals against your skin. It covered both sides of the house with a small iron door in the middle.

Once you unlocked the latch on the iron door, you were in the court yard. Now, it sort of reminds me of one of those houses you see in southern California with the sizable back yard, but it's not really a back yard with grass and a pool.

The floor is tiled – a sort of Moroccan tile with warm peach, steel blue, and shiny gray colors. You can choose to go to the right where you will find three orange trees and three lemon trees, before you wrap around the house and see the back yard with grapes and figs growing above in the outdoor garden. Or you could go left and see the door to the basement filled with random shit, before you wrap around the other side of the house and see the little chicken and rooster coop or hen house – whatever it's called.

Now, let's walk to the front of the house again. You climb up the few concrete stairs and you are on the front porch, complete with a little nook to sit or read. You can grab oranges from the front porch by the way. I told you – happiness.

Through the double, front doors you enter inside to a large square entry way. On the left are two doors; one is the living room and one is a bedroom. On the right, there are two doors; my grandparents' bedroom and the bathroom. Straight across the front door is the door to the chill sitting area or I guess a family room. You walk through the family room to get to the kitchen. My favorite.

My average day consisted of getting up around eight and washing up, before I ran outside and grabbed all the eggs the chickens had laid. My grandmother made the best vezë të skuqura (fried eggs) – see another easy food description. She threw in some feta cheese when she fried them....so good. I want to make some right now, but I'll continue making you jealous with descriptions.

Also! She would get up around six in the morning and go get fresh baked bread at the bakery. I told you – it's like a once upon a time story.

Breakfast is still my favorite meal of the day.

We would then go to the market – together. It was a daily occurrence. You know when you're in college or even recently graduated or even all the moms out there and that one white girl you know (she may be your friend too) excitedly tells you she went to a farmer's market that weekend. Bitch, please.

Every day was the farmer's market for me. If you have ever been to a farmer's market you know what I'm talking about. If not, it's basically an outdoor market, with tents and everything, where they sell produce, fruit, nuts, etc. You got everything there as there was no Whole Foods around the corner where you could pick up some green peppers you forgot for your dinner recipe.

And there is negotiating – lots of it and my grandma was the champ of deals. She would always score the best cherries for me, since she knew they were my favorite and still are.

It was my favorite part – the market, because on the way there, my grandma and I would decide what we were going to eat that day for lunch and dinner. There was no preplan or need to know everything so far ahead. It was thrilling – remember that for later.

After the market, we would go back home and water the plants, clean the house, hang out with the neighbors and so on before we began cooking. My grandma cooked, and I watched. She never used recipes and she's the reason I don't need them either.

It was a beautiful time. Clean summer air, fresh fruit, sunshine, friendly neighbors, not a worry in mind.

You get the idea and I'm pretty sure you would want to be there too.

Why the overly descriptive elements of the house and my daily schedule?

Here's a fact I have come to know over the years; you tend to miss the details when you are happy. You don't think much about it – you're just happy living in the moment until you're not. When you are sad you remember every striking detail, every soul damaging moment and every time your heart jumps to your throat.

Remember when I told you my father was not the first man I loved?

You notice how I keep saying my grandparents' house, but I did not once mention my grandfather?

My grandfather acted the way my father should have when I was born. He had a weak spot for me – my parents named me after his mother, aka my great grandmother, and it worked out great because technically my name is a combination of my parents' name as well.

My grandfather was also the poster boy for not judging a book by its cover or stereotyping people. He was a truck driver – mostly import export freight in neighboring countries, though he did go to France one time. Additionally, he had a motor cycle – not a bitch bike or Vespa. It was a Harley type of motor cycle.

Your mind just went to a bad boy, smoking, and breaking hearts while wearing a leather jacket – mine did too.

You would think, my grandfather was rough and probably old fashioned considering most of his life was under Hoxha's rule. You would think he would treat my grandmother poorly, his daughter like property, and act like a complete condescending douche.

Well you would be wrong.

The house, I described so precisely earlier – he built that for my grandma. When my grandma could no longer work due to health complications – he worked twice as hard to make sure they had everything they needed. When the decision came for him to allow my mother to get married – he did not hesitate to make it her decision.

Pause.

What do I mean *allowed* my mom to get married?

Albanians have this hierarchy thing. My mom is the third child and her older sister had not been married which meant without my grandfather's permission my mom would not get married either.

41

In case you were wondering – I'm not a fan of the whole asking for my hand in marriage thing. Even if I had the most spectacular relationship with my father, let me remind you that you are marrying ME, not my father and he can't ever make that decision for me. I decide to share a house, a bed and my life with you, NOT my father.

Also, for those quote on quote traditional people out there – here's a quick history lesson for you. The reason a man asks your father for your hand in marriage is because back in the good old days, women were property. Hence why you take a man's last name – to become his property. I don't say this to hate on all the people who have taken their husband's last names – good for you. I say this for all the people others make feel bad for their decision not to take their husband's last name. The only reason others look at you sideways is because you are an individual, and you don't fit into the social mold others have created. Keep doing you.

End of rant.

My grandfather told my mom it was her decision, not his. My grandfather was the one who told my mom that if she continued to hit my sister, he would not visit anymore. (Yes, we got hit as children) My grandfather was the one who never made me feel like I was a disappointment because I was a girl. I was just his grandchild, and he didn't care if I was a girl or boy – he just wanted to see me live and be happy.

That caring, gentle, supportive, and loving man is the one I fell in love with first.

So, why did it take me 25 years to realize I should just be myself if I had such a shining example as a child?

Because life isn't fair…actually that's the truth, but it's cheesy. Here's the real reason:

Brain Cancer.

It was a day like every other day at the house. My grandparents' house. The only difference were the people. So many people in one house. I didn't think about it much – I was four years old. My mom told me my grandfather wanted a glass of water and I was confused. Why was she making me get it?

My grandmother was one of the strongest women I had ever known. Funny too – everybody says I'm just like her, but we will get to that later. I had never felt hands shaking as violently as hers were when she helped me fill the glass with water. She knew what was coming.

They say, when someone has Alzheimer's they forget their newest memories first.

Well, let me be the one to tell you, brain cancer is the ultimate bitch. She not only makes you forget who people are, but if she progresses as much as she had in my grandfather's brain – she makes you forget basic life functions like how to eat. She makes you forget utensils are supposed to go in your mouth and not on your feet. She makes you forget when you were born. She makes you forget who you are. Somehow though, she can never erase your soul.

When I walked into my grandparents' room, where my grandfather was lying down, I was confused – again. So many people. I handed him the glass of water and he took it and just looked at me with a small smile resting on his lips, but I noticed his eyes the most. Such love, such pride – an invisible sparkle.

You never really pay attention to the way people look at you, and you only are reminded of it when you are watching a cheesy movie. It's always a dramatic scene in a Nicholas Sparks movie in which the girl yells, "You never look at me how you look at her!"

Girl, how would you know how he is looking at you? Ugh...

This will bite me in the ass later. Hollywood is responsible for these high expectations.

My grandfather had forgotten a lot, but the way he looked at me, the way he smiled sadly – it was like he knew my heart, like he was trying to tell me that while life may be extremely unfair and difficult, it will never be able to take away the beauty and love of a soul.

That was it. One moment there was a sparkle and the next there was nothing. It was not silent, by the way – Albanians and especially old women have a thing about wailing when someone dies. The louder, the more they feel like they are mourning properly. My grandma was not wailing by the way. It was some distant cousins and nobody I recognized.

If you are wondering about how Albanians handle death – it's not pretty, but that's a story for another chapter. As far as kids are concerned – parents don't tell their child someone when to the sky or went away for a while, or went to heaven.

They died. End of story.

Harsh? Maybe, but we are simple, remember?

They were breathing and now they aren't.

Simple.

I was four. I had no idea what death meant, but I knew my grandfather was not coming back anytime soon. I sat in the family room the whole day. People walked in, walked out, but I just sat there. I didn't cry. I didn't move. I didn't speak. I didn't even watch TV. I just stared at my hands. It was my first practice at internalizing, and dear God it only gets worse.

Lesson of the Chapter

Cherish happy memories, no matter how small or simple they may seem at the time.

CHAPTER 5

Neighborhood Boys

This is probably the chapter you think I tell you some sort of juicy stories about childhood crushes and late nights in the streets of Albania.

Sorry. Think again.

Also, perv – are you forgetting I was eight when I moved to the States?

Also, also, writing is hard. I mean, I already knew that, but damn. It's Saturday now and I've completed five chapters (technically – if you include the epilogue). That's 10,000 words and my neck hurts, but sacrifices must be made when testing a theory.

Whew.

You know that hot button topic? Not fitting in? Let's get back to that.

Have you ever sat down after a break up – thought back to everything that happened and suddenly the break up makes sense? You could swear he was there for you, but you can't think of one time he actually made an effort without you telling him too? Or how you remember him saying you look beautiful, but he actually said you look hot?

Side Bar. I know what all the guys are thinking.

Jesus. Is this how girls think? What's wrong with saying she looks hot?

Here is a simple, but painless piece of advice boys.

From Albania, With Love

You tell a one night stand she's hot, but you tell your girlfriend she looks beautiful. Just like you call your "side piece" baby, instead of her given name, because you are afraid you might slip up and call her your girlfriend's name. Even if you don't want to make her your girlfriend – you should still call her beautiful, because being a gentleman is always a great idea.

You're welcome.

So, as I was saying – that's what this is. I am looking back, realizing that I was not really set up to succeed in the being myself or feeling loved department when I was young. It is making me realize why I am the way I am. It's a bird's eye view of my life, so no pity from you.

When I thought back to it, I remember three things (amongst many others). To make this painless, I will format them like an appendix.

Exhibit A: My cousins.

I have a big family – I already told you this. Most of the size comes from my father's side. Remember the whole boy girl, thousands of cousins thing?

Well, when we would go on vacation or play at my grandmother's house (my dad's mom), it was always all the cousins and we were all around the same age. I was the youngest of the pack. I'm sure I have some fellow younger siblings or youngest in a group of friends out there reading this, so you can agree with me that it sort of sucks.

Most families defend the youngest – they can make fun of you, but nobody else can. As you saw with Berta – I could clearly take care of myself, but it still sort of stings. You want people to be protective of you, you want to play with the big kids, you don't want to be chosen last for someone's basketball team on the playground, you want to be spoiled like the youngest usually is. Well, my family didn't care.

Tough love, I guess.

I don't know if you have ever watched Sailor Moon. It was a cartoon back in the day, about a group of girls with powers – they each represented a planet. It was my favorite show, and because we did not have iPhones and iPads to play with, we role played.

Nope. Don't let your mind go to weird places. We were kids.

It was sort of like Comic-Con without the costumes. We would just run around the neighborhood and reenact the episode we had just seen. Now, I know I said it was a show in which all the characters were girls, but we did not discriminate on the playground so, one of our boy cousins would join us. The leader of the pack was our eldest cousin and she always chose to be the main character and we said nothing – hierarchy.

Since, I said real people, fake names – my cousins will be named after the characters they role played when we were young. I will not bother with ALL the cousins. Just the exclusive play group we had.

Sailor Moon – The eldest cousin…She did have the hair length of Sailor Moon.

From Albania, With Love

Sailor Mercury – My sister…She had a weird obsession with the ocean.

Sailor Mars – A cousin the same age as my sister…I don't know anybody who has experimented with as much hair dye as she has.

Sailor Jupiter – A cousin two years younger than my sister… She had a more extreme bowl cut than I did.

Sailor Venus – My boy cousin… It's weird to think he is in a serious relationship now.

Anybody who has seen Sailor Moon will tell you that they only had five sailor girls. So, where does that leave me?

I was the mascot. Sailor Moon had a trusty cat sidekick. Yes, he was very important to the story and he could talk which was pretty cool, but he was a cat.

I don't like cats.

Back then I was happy to be playing, but now – bird's eye view – it sucked! I didn't get to transform into a cool imaginary costume, I didn't get to fight the bad guys, I didn't get to have a made-up love interest and all I really wanted was to be Sailor Jupiter. I mean she could electrocute people, she was a tomboy, and she was a brunette!

Hello!

I know I should not be this sensitive about this, but we couldn't make my boy cousin the male cat? Really?

Talk about being left out. I was picked to be the fucking mascot.

Exhibit B: My uncle.

I know what this story is going to sound like, so I need you to focus.

My sister was not only popular in the friend department, she was also popular in the boys' department – she still is. She has an ease about her, it's simple to get to know her. She is emotional (not in a bad way), she'll tell you what's bothering her, she'll communicate and she is beautiful.

When she was about nine or ten, there was this guy in her class who had a crush on her. If I can remember correctly – he was very easy on the eyes and chill! I know he was just a kid, but he was one of those kids that you know are going to grow up to break hearts because they know they can. Bad boy type.

Anyway, remember when I told you a people person type of person is also appeasing? Well, our Sailor Moon cousin liked this boy – let's call him James. The same one who liked my sister and they all went to the same school.

The drama of it all!

Sailor Moon would drag our little cousin – unnamed – down to the playground just so James would notice her and talk to her. At school, she would make sure to be close to James and especially at lunch. No bite from James – apparently, he liked it when girls played hard to get.

Of course, my sister was not playing – she was appeasing. She ignored James because Sailor Moon liked him and my sister did not want a confrontation or to be kicked out of the playing group.

Ah... the simplicities of childhood.

From Albania, With Love

As much as my sister tried, James was right there. He cut lines at school to be near her. He would only go to the playground with his younger brother when my sister was there, and he made a point to walk home with her after school...every day.

He was determined – I'll give him that.

What does this have to do with my uncle & me?

One day, after school, my uncle noticed my sister was upset. This is my father's youngest brother by the way – it was his young son my sister would take to the playground. Just like I spent time on my mom's side, my sister spent most of her childhood on my dad's side.

Wanting to avoid confrontation, my sister told my uncle that a boy at school was bothering her.

On every apartment block in Fier, there were these garbage cans. They were actually more like those dumpsters you see in the back of a restaurant or café. Everybody threw their trash there and once a week it would be cleaned and emptied.

I don't know if you know where this is going, but I'll tell you.

The day after my sister told our uncle a boy was bothering her, she was once again walking home from school with James next to her. My uncle very calmly walked down to where they were coming from and proceeded to grab James by his collar. Anger probably laced his voice when he told James never to talk to his niece again if he knew what was best for him. Then, he proceeded to throw James in the dumpster.

Poor James.

I know what you are going to say.

So... you are jealous your sister can get attention from guys? You are jealous your uncle did the most to protect her? You are blaming your sister?

No. Yes. No.

That protective characteristic I have? It sort of burns when you realize you grew that extra spine when you were so young, because you never had anybody stand up for you the way you stood up for them. Don't get me wrong, I am sure my family would have stood up for me if I had a boy bothering me, and I don't need anybody to stand up for me – I can handle myself – but it's still nice to have that safe haven.

Exhibit C: Vacation.

Last one – I promise.

I don't know how to swim.

I know. I know. Don't make a mistake though. If you throw me in the middle of the ocean, I will survive. I will not be very happy about it, but I will be fine.

Usually – in Albania, a child learns how to swim when the family goes on vacation. The beaches are magnificent. We are on the Mediterranean Sea after all.

The same uncle who threw James in the trash was going on vacation one summer with a few other family members, and most of the Sailor Moon cousins. They were going to this magnificent place down south called Qeparo. It has the clearest body of sea you will ever see. When the sun hits the top layer, it's like gems dancing on the water. Look it up – you'll thank me later.

I was young so I don't remember a lot, but when I heard about it, I was so excited. I mean what kid doesn't get excited about the beach, and especially a vacation without their parents telling them what to do?

The next memory I have of that summer is standing in the middle of the street watching the car take off for vacation with my sister inside. Sort of like that heart-breaking moment in a movie when a kid is watching his parents drive off to go put their dog down. I know – super dramatic, and again as a kid I was sad for about two seconds. I hung out with my grandma that summer and now I wish I had appreciated that more.

Just put yourself in my shoes though. My sister learned to swim that summer and I got left out. Again.

Red hot button issue. Just make sure to remember these exhibits for later – trust me, they will explain a lot of my behavior and my recent epiphanies.

Lesson of the Chapter

If you want to move forward, you have to look back.

CHAPTER 6

Diversity Act

U sually when you tell people you won the lottery, they think you've made it. You're rich. No need to ever work again. They may even try to be your friend to get a piece of the action. When I tell people I won the lottery to come to the United States they usually have one of the following three responses;

1. So, you won the lottery then you used the money to come to the States?

2. Wait…. You feel so lucky to be here, you consider it winning the lottery?

3. What…?

Now that we've gotten all the childhood stuff out of the way – sort of – let me fill you in on how I am able to sit here, in Massachusetts writing my alleged life story.

…. *Pause* ….

Okay, I'm back. Didn't notice I was gone? Well, I had to go to CVS and get an IcyHot patch because my neck is killing me. Now my neck smells like old people. Sexy, I know.

The occupational hazards of being a writer.

Back to the story.

In case you haven't noticed America is very white. Sometimes it's blindingly white. I don't mean the color, I mean the people. People born and raised here for centuries can't have a broad sense of the world. They can't necessarily think outside of the box or compare and contrast. If you're offended by that statement, now you know how every immigrant feels when they are stereotyped, and it's usually much worse for us.

The problem is that unless you are exposed to different ideas – you can never come up with new ones, which can help advance your life, or your country or just everything over all. Too much vanilla for too long can make your taste buds go flat.

It's the reason why couples try out role playing, it's the reason why parents try a new parenting method when their kid is being a dipshit, it's the reason why NASA had to bring women on to their staff, and it's the reason why the great United States of America established the Immigrant Diversity Act in 1990.

They looked in the mirror and the reflection was white as fuck. They were not advancing in any sector. They were stuck, so they ventured out in the world.

For all the racists pricks reading this – I don't know why you even picked this book up, but I know what you are saying.

So what if we are white? This is our country and we will be whatever we want. We don't need anybody's help.

Newsflash, asshole: This is *NOT* your country. Everybody is an immigrant to this country. Pick up a fucking history book. AND, next time you want to tell me or anybody else that you want your country back, actually take a second to think about what is spilling from your foul mouth and figure out your hateful issues elsewhere, because we aren't going anywhere, and you should thank us for that.

Why, you ask?

Google – Co-founded by a Russian born computer scientist.

Hot Dogs – Created by a German immigrant.

YouTube – Co-founded by a German immigrant, an American, and an American of Taiwanese descent.

Ketchup – Created by the son of a German immigrant.

Apple – Founded by the son of a Syrian refugee.

Donuts – Created by a refugee from Russia.

Hamburgers – Created by a Danish immigrant.

"God Bless America" (Song) – Written by a Jewish immigrant from Belarus.

The White House – Designed by an architect who immigrated from Ireland.

Chevrolet Motor Car Company – Founded by a man born in Switzerland, raised in France, and lived in Canada before moving to America.

Jeans – Created by a German immigrant.

So, you want your country back? Say goodbye to the most "American" things I have ever known – blue jeans, hot dogs, ketchup, Chevy cars, and the White House.

Yeah, you're welcome.

Let's get back on track.

What is the Immigrant Diversity Act of 1990?

From Albania, With Love

It's a lottery!

Each year, the US makes 50,000 permanent resident visas (green cards) available to be distributed around the world. Based on the census taken each year, they determine how many will be available in the participating countries. For example, if there are only a few Albanians in the US, more visas will be available in Albania that specific year; if there is a heavy abundance of Taiwanese people in the US, there will be less visas distributed to Taiwan. However, no country ever gets more than 3,500 each year – to make it fair, I guess.

What qualifies a person to apply for the lottery?

An applicant has to be a high school graduate. They must have no criminal background, and they must be in good health. Oh, and they have to be 18 years old. The saddest part was when a family would get selected for the lottery but they could not bring their kids because they were 18 or older.

Everybody, and I mean everybody in Albania wanted to come to the United States. Remember our friend Hoxha?

Well, during his rule, he told people the western world was the devil because…freedom – of course. So, when people were free and able to come to the US, they were thrilled to get a chance to experience this great nation everybody talks about.

Rumors spread worse than a wildfire in Albania. The US was the land of opportunity, the land of excellent education for children, the land of freedom, the land of possibilities. It was everything. Over the years, those who immigrated to the US, did not help calm those flaming rumors down. It's not that they aren't true, but people stretched the truth to seem like the best version of themselves, and the people in Albania thought the US was a walk in the park. I will elaborate very soon – I promise.

Fate is a funny thing. Some people believe in it and some think it's bullshit. I believe in it – not in a blinding way, because sometimes people are just stupid. Like when I was in college and my friend told me that her and her boyfriend are meant to be – it was fate.

No, bitch. It was you. You forgave him after he cheated on you. Twice.

I believe in fate when something uncontrollable happens. When you put all your cards down or play all the hands you have, and then something happens.

My mom filled out the paper work for the Lottery and my dad sleepily signed the bottom line. As my mom went to the post office to hand the papers in, she was not even sure they would accept them since my dad botched his signature, but away they went and we waited.

I mean, I wasn't waiting – I didn't even know what the Lottery really was when I was younger. From what I had heard, America was this phantom country in which everybody was happy and always got what they wanted. A magical place that doesn't really exist – sort of like Narnia.

You know when I was telling you we never remember details when we are happy?

From Albania, With Love

Well, worse than that, we never really know how much influence something – a person, place, experience, time, etc. – will have on us later. I know all my fellow writers, singers, and artists out there understand what I am saying.

Maybe, I'm not making any sense to anybody, but what I am basically saying is that I never thought I was special. I never thought fate had a grand plan for me and I know I shouldn't have – I was a kid, but I went on thinking I was just another person on this earth until about two years ago. And, no I don't suddenly think I can save everybody now, but I have a voice. I have a story. The lottery was the starting point for me. Even though I didn't have the slightest idea, fate was already pushing me.

I promise it will make sense in a few chapters.

I think you can probably guess that I don't like math, but I did do some math recently. Here are the statistics based on the numbers from that year's Lottery:

0.00000007% chance of being selected in the pool of applicants in the world.

0.0000005% chance of being selected in the pool of applicants in Albania.

If that's not fate, I don't know what is.

Migena Dulaj

Lesson of the Chapter

Fate takes action. Let her steer you in the right
direction.

CHAPTER 7

October 26th, 2000 – 11:30PM

I'm not a celebrity. Clearly.

I don't know what it's like to get followed around with cameras. I don't know what it's like to feel out of control – like you don't know who might jump out at you. I don't know what it's like to have people revere you like you are God's gift to earth. I don't know what it's like to be hated by nations of people, though I am sure a few people dislike me or hate me. I don't know what it's like to have a team of people getting me ready in the morning or planning my schedule.

I think you get the point.

I do, however, know the feeling that surges through your veins when everybody thinks you have just completely made it in life and you have no fucking idea what they are on about.

The time after my dad's name was drawn for the Lottery is a giant blur in my memory. Being selected did not necessarily mean you got to just hop on a plane and be on your way. My parents had to go to Greece to appear at the Albanian embassy for the interview since the embassy in Albania was closed due to some crazy protest or something. They thought they were only going to be there for about two days, but they ended up staying for two weeks. The problem was my dad's high school diploma.

Now, here is the part about honesty that I will commit to.

You recall my dad is the eldest in his family?

Well, my dad started working when he was about 14 years old to support his family and his then young sisters. All the money he made went to the family and yes, he did go to school but he had to find something he was good at, something he could commit to that allowed him to make extra cash. He picked cars.

To this day, my dad is a world class, self-taught mechanic who can figure out any car, any model, any year, any problem. To answer your question, yes – it does come in handy. I have never gone to the auto shop to fix my car because I have my own personal mechanic.

You are also probably thinking: Well, why didn't his parents work to support the family? They did, but during Hoxha's rule, food was distributed by rations, each week or so. I know, it sounds like a young adult dystopian world (hint, hint). The government didn't particularly give a shit if you had one kid or ten kids. So, it was up to the families to have more money to feed their kids.

What's my point?

My point is that my dad wasn't the best student in high school and it wasn't because he was stupid – it was because he didn't have time to apply himself, but he is very resourceful. It's one of the things which I have come to realize over the years. He will always find a way, even if it's the hard way.

From Albania, With Love

Because he didn't have time to study or even show up to school, my dad did favors. His teachers needed their car fixed – my dad fixed it in one day. His teachers needed rides to the capital or outlying villages – my dad was their driver. Legal? Probably not, but he got his diploma.

When my parents went to Greece, they took a new copy of the diploma because they had lost the old one in the shuffle of moving into our apartment with the shotty construction. The embassy thought it was a fake, because as they claimed – it was too new. It should have been old and the color should have been stripped.

Tools.

After some highly tense days, my parents got their visa and we were off! On our way to America.

Hold up.

In reality, we actually had to go get checked. They had to ensure we were all healthy enough to pass the physical exam. It wasn't some sort of fucked up physical test in which we had to run the mile or anything, but still I remember being nervous. I don't remember the physical exam – selective memories I guess – but I remember the walk there. My mom was reassuring me that it would be fine, which actually did not really help, because let's be honest, you only ever tell someone it will be okay when you have no fucking idea how it will end.

It will be okay is sort of like when someone says they are fine. As a champion user of the phrase "I'm fine" I can guarantee you, nothing is fine when those words slip out of your mouth.

Anyway, back to the point.

Remember that feeling I was telling you about? When you feel dazed because everybody is so excited for you, but you have no idea why?

The morning of October 26, 2000, I was in a daze.

I woke up. Washed my face. Brushed my teeth. Pulled up my Calvin Klein jeans and threw on my thick wool sweater and then I stood in the hallway across the front door of my parents' apartment. Everybody was there. Uncles, aunts, grandparents, Sailor Moon cousins, friends, people I didn't recognize. I could hear my family discussing where our things would go, who would take the books, the couch, the dishes.

I understood enough to know we were moving, but I didn't know why, I didn't really understand people's excitement, I didn't really pay attention to my parents when they told us a simple version of the plan, and I certainly didn't understand why my mom was crying, but she knew what I didn't or maybe what I chose not to think of.

We would never move back.

We would never be home again.

We would technically be alone.

Completely out of our comfort zones.

Surrounded by strange people.

A language none of us understood even the slightest bit.

From Albania, With Love

Somewhere in their heart, though, my parents had blinding hope that something better was waiting for us even if it was in a foreign land, and even if they had to sacrifice their life for their kids.

When someone gets married in Albania, it's a three-day long affair. A story for another time, but basically one day is spent at the groom's house, one day is spent at the bride's, and the last day is together – the families joining together. There is so much more to it than that, but the point is, I obviously didn't attend my parents' wedding, but I was there when my uncle got married. You know – the one who threw James in the trash.

Well, when I say the whole neighborhood comes out to watch the bride descend from the apartment building and get into the car to go celebrate the wedding, I mean it's like a small version of a British royal wedding. It always felt like the whole city gathered there, especially since apartments were structured in clusters.

One little cluster could have five or six apartment buildings with more than 40 families in each building. People went to the courtyard. People hung over the balconies. People looked out their windows. People cheered. People took photos. It was the closest we got to celebrity fandom.

When I finally descended down those same stairs I split my head open on, my eyes didn't really know where to look first. It was like a wedding. All the neighbors knew we were going to America. They were observing us, looking at us with jealousy, interest, and awe. It was strange, but again, as a kid I don't remember anything but my family kissing my cheeks until they felt like they would fall off.

The blurriness of that day is filled with sharp clear memories which last about 30 seconds each. It was the first time I got on a plane, but the only thing I remember is my dad crying when we arrived to JFK.

No, he wasn't crying because he was so happy to be in the US. He was crying because he missed his family.

Side Bar.

For those of you out there that think it's weak for a boy or man to cry, I don't agree with you. You want to know why? Here's a scientific reason. Men are human too.

Wow.

Crying is good for the soul. Trust me.

I remember asking my mom if my dad was okay and do you know what she said?

He's fine.

Right.

JFK was not our final destination – Logan International was.

Have you ever been to some place – outside the US – and you literally have no idea what is going on? No idea what people are saying. No idea why even the people look different. Have you then been there again and it felt a little more familiar, not as strange?

If this has not happened to you – let me tell you, that strange feeling will never fade. You will always remember it, you will always remember the introduction to something. Sort of like first impressions.

That's how Boston was for me on Thursday, October 26th, 2000. It was the first time I had ever stepped foot on American soil and every time I go to Logan, I remember that night.

No matter the time of day, I remember the sparkling lights from the Boston skyline at 11:30PM. No matter the weather, I remember the chilly, rain soaked terminal E road with just the slightest bit of October breeze blowing around me. No matter how busy, I remember the dead stillness of the approaching midnight hour.

Hey, are you still there?

I hope so, because remember those embarrassing elementary and middle school stories everybody has?

Well, imagine being the weird kid from an alleged third world country.

Hold tight kids. Shame is headed your way.

Lesson of the Chapter

You never forget a first impression.

CHAPTER 8

1st Day of School

I've always had a problem with Disney.

No, not Disney Channel – I actually watched that shit in college. What I have a problem with is Walt Disney World or Disneyland (take your pick). It's like this elusive place. The happiest place on earth. Yeah, happiest, if you enjoy screaming kids, disgustingly sticky weather, over priced tickets, and aggravated parents. I know the exact phrase running through your head right now.

What a bitch!

Here's the thing. I've never been to either Disneyland or Walt Disney World. Would I like to go? Sure. Didn't I just say I have a problem with it? Sure.

My real problem is with the parents. The parents that take their one year old or two-year-old to Disney. Your kid will not remember shit! If you are going because you like it, then go for it, but don't use your kid as the excuse. You want to know how I know the kid will not remember a thing? Every single friend I had in college or high school who had been to Disney when they were younger – like 7 and below – only remembered they went because they had photos or the Mickey ears.

Why am I ranting about Disney?

Because learning English is my Disney. I don't remember how I did it.

From Albania, With Love

The most common fascination people have about me is the fact that I didn't speak a word of English before I moved here. My sister took a few English lessons when we were in Albania, but I never did, and when I say I don't remember how I learned English, I don't actually mean that part is completely blank and void.

I was in the third grade when we moved to the States – rough, I know. The town I live in has, what feels like, a billion elementary schools. Okay, actually – there are only six, but in Fier, Albania there was one. One city, one elementary school.

You know when your mom says she bought you and your brother that new, shiny toy you had both been wanting? You are both so excited. A perfect, new, thrilling toy is on the way to you. Then she comes home with the new toy, but it's not the one you wanted. It's not perfect. It's ugly and strange looking and you don't understand it.

That is what being an immigrant child feels like. You can see the disappointment in people's faces when the teacher announces the new student is from Albania – a place people haven't the slightest idea about. A place that somehow, people think is part of Russia. A place in which people don't even know what language is spoken. And a place in which, apparently, girls have extreme short hair. I still had the bowl cut.

Instead of being the cool kid from France or England – or hell, even some fucking made up place like Genovia – I was the kid from the scary country with the aggressive double headed eagle on the flag. The country which produced villains in movies and books. The country represented as struggling and poor. The communist country.

Also, if you think it got better – like somehow people magically got educated the older I got – you would be absolutely wrong.

First day of school?

Total fucking blur.

I obviously speak English now, but when the teacher paired me with a girl – let's call her Kate – I had no idea what she was saying. Thinking back on it now, I still don't know what she was saying, because like I told you, learning English was my Disney. I remember going to lessons and classes, but I don't remember when I learned that a window is a window or that paper is paper.

Side Bar.

I don't know why people assume that when someone doesn't speak English, they will suddenly understand you if you speak slowly and loudly. We won't and you will just sound fucking ignorant. Stop it.

Back on track.

You know that Taylor Swift lyrics when she says:

"Forgetting him is like trying to know someone you never met"

Well, that's English. I can't remember a specific time when I knew how to speak, read, and write in perfect English. Don't get me wrong, I still get tripped up sometimes and grammar is far from my favorite topic, even though

From Albania, With Love

English was always my favorite subject in school. Remember that simplicity Albanians have?

Yeah, well I still call things how they are and my college roommates always got a laugh out of it. I would say shit like; I watched a dream or I am closing the lights. That's okay, because English will always be my second language and I am happy about that.

Just in case you were wondering – I learned English in about six months. I guess that's what happens when you are a kid and you have no fear, doubt, stress or anxiety clouding your brain.

I would be lying to you if I said there weren't some expressions and words which were scarring to the whole experience of learning English.

Don't believe me? Okay.

By definition a car in the English language is a vehicle moving on wheels. Simple enough. A kar in the Albanian language is a dick.

Yep. You read that right.

So, now imagine someone saying the following to you:

Do you want a ride in my car?
How much mileage does your car have?
Is it a new or used car?

I'll stop. You get the idea – the jokes are endless, but hey, there's a new word for you girls and guys out there to use, discreetly, if you want to discuss a topic that's not so appropriate in public. See, knowing another language is fun and useful. Not that I have to tell you that, considering the most common request I receive is to teach Albanian swear words. It usually doesn't end well. We have 36 letters, remember?

Back to the story. Elementary school.

To be completely truthful, it wasn't all too bad. At least before I knew what people were saying. Is ignorance really bliss?

I know the times have changed over the years. I know that bullies are still around, but I think people my age and older will agree with me that the way bullies were handled when we were in school was much less aggressive. If there were words exchanged between two students – they both got sent to the principal's office. If one kid got teased, he/she never really said anything, because kids will be kids, right? And I mean, who wants to be that sensitive kid that complains.

In school, especially before college, people are one of two things; the bully or the victim. And I know victim is a strong word, but go with me. If you were the victim, or even if you minded your own business, you will still remember that one person who was the major bully or popular girl/guy.

Mine was the popular girl – let's call her Penny.

Penny was petite. She had pin straight, dirty blonde hair, and small glasses that somehow still looked good on her. She was not your usual mean girl who isn't the most intelligent, instead she was adored by all the teachers, and she was always at the top of the scoring chart when we had

72

exams. I mean – we were in elementary school. It wasn't advanced placement English. That's a whole other story.

Penny was not like Kate. Remember Kate? She was nice, inclusive – didn't make me feel like an outsider. She is actually a teacher now which is sort of ironic, but anyways back to Penny. Bottom line; the girls wanted to be Penny and the boys wanted to hang out with Penny.

Just like Penny was book smart, she also knew what she had to do so everybody continued to like her, because apparently, she had never heard of just being nice with no motive. After I could communicate and actually hold a conversation, she invited me to sit at her table at lunch. I know – this sounds like some scene out of Mean Girls.

There are a lot of mysteries one must uncover when moving to a new culture and country and for most immigrants, I can guarantee, it was packed lunches. I don't think my mom had ever packed me a lunch before we came to the states. In Albania, my grandma's house was so close, I would go home for lunch. It was a hell of a lot better than school lunches.

What did my mom pack me?

Two boiled eggs. The thickest slice of homemade bread you have ever seen. Feta cheese. A hot dog – just the sausage part. An orange. A banana.

I know exactly what sort of face you are making right now. Disgusted. And, yes, you can only imagine the smell the boiled eggs and sausages emitted.

Penny sat through that lunch, but I could tell from all the glares and whispers escaping from her lips – I would not be invited again. It did not stop there.

You know when a kid sees his mom do something, so he does it to?

Well, that's how mean girl groups work. Kate continued to sit with me, when she could, but everybody else followed Penny's lead in calling me weird when they didn't think I was listening, in spreading weird rumors about where I was from, in gossiping about my non-English speaking parents, in commenting about the way I dressed, and at one point one of them went to the teacher and told her that I had flakes in my hair. Yes, I'll admit it – I had dandruff, but my shampoo was just not agreeing with me.

My teacher sent me to the nurse and the nurse wanted to call my parents and explain the situation. She also wanted to have my vaccination charts, just in case I was not spreading some sort of third world country disease on the white kids of America. I told her that my parents were working and that I would give them her message.

What would I really do?

I would deal with it, I would not bother my parents with some stupid shit, and lastly, I would never put my parents in that uncomfortable situation. Especially when the nurse stated her sentence with:

"Well, in this country…"

I was young, so I didn't think much about it, but thinking back on it now…

Dear God, my hand is twitching with the need to back hand her across the face.

After that, the charades continued, because as my luck would have it – we were literally the only family from anywhere to move to this white town in Massachusetts. It got to the point when one of Penny's little tag alongs told me to go back to where I came from.

Creative – really.

Thinking back now, I would have probably told her that at least I have somewhere to go back to, but again, I was young and I wanted to fit in… there is that hot topic button again. After that comment, I would still take the lunch my mom would pack for me, but when I got to school I would throw it out, and I think it was the guiltiest I have ever felt in my childhood.

You see, while, yes, technically we weren't poor in Albania, I still knew people – distant family members that lacked food, and the time my mom took to make my lunch was also wasted and that just wasn't fair, considering everything else she was doing.

Before, we move to any other chapters, I need you to understand something.

Without exception, children who immigrate to the United States are all affected by the immigrant child syndrome.

What is that?

It's not a medical condition – relax.

It's all the elements, characteristics, actions, and occurrences that mold an immigrant to become who they are in life. In this case, I don't mean when you tell me your parents are from here and there or that you are part this and part that. I don't need your oh so exotic background, because guess what? It will always just be a background! Saying you are part Croatian doesn't tell me shit. It literally only tells me that your physical attributes are due to a diverse DNA pool.

Coming to America. English being your second language. Dealing with extremely different surroundings than the ones you were raised in. Being a parent to your parents. Growing a thick skin to insults, stereotypes, and bullies. Feeling guilty when you aren't good enough. Wanting to be perfect. Having an extremely difficult time figuring out who you are. Constantly trying to fit in somewhere. Internalizing.

These are immigrant child syndrome side effects. It will make a lot more sense in the college years, but just keep it in mind.

Lesson of the Chapter

Don't ever change what makes you different.

CHAPTER 9

$8.30 Available Balance

The first time I touched snow, I was eight years old. Yes, there are regions in Albania in the north where it snows, but I lived in the southern region. I remember I was walking home from the school bus stop and it started snowing. It was obviously cold, and contrary to what most people think – no, I was not accustomed to the cold as I told you, Albania is not near Russia.

I like the way snow looks on trees – it makes beautiful scenery. Beautiful in the sort of – I'm in a cozy ass cabin, drinking delicious hot chocolate and enjoying the view – type of way. When it comes down to it, I really don't like dealing with it. It's cold. It's miserable. It makes for torturous driving conditions. AND, I seriously think I am having a heart attack every time I have to shovel.

The first house we had when we moved to the States wasn't really a house. Well – it was, but we lived in the roof like we were the fucking mice in Cinderella. It had a bedroom, bathroom, kitchen and living room, but don't kid yourself – you could get from one side to the other in less than five seconds.

My sister and I had a makeshift bedroom in the living room, so when we had guests over, they would sit on our made-up beds. When I went to bed, if I held my hand out,

I could touch the ceiling due to the slant in the roof. It was not ideal, but hey, at least we were in America, right?

Why did we live there?

The most important thing to have when selected for the Diversity Immigrant Visa is a contact in the US. A person or family you know is best, because this person will guide you – they will show you what to do, which town is best to live in, how to spend your money, where to shop. To make this list short, let's just say they basically show you how to live in this strange country you know close to nothing about.

You know how they say some people just want to watch the world burn? Well, keep that in mind.

My parents didn't really have any contacts or people they knew in the United States, but one of my dad's sisters had a close friend. Let's call them the Brown family.

The Brown family had been living just outside of Boston for a few years – I think it was something like ten or 12 years. They were like those overly hyped people... overly friendly on the brink of crazy type of people. Almost too eager to help, but not listen to what we wanted because I guess they figured we didn't know any better.

If you haven't figured it out by now – my family was very traditional. I know my, sometimes foul mouth may not make it seem like that but to this day I have not had the sex talk with my parents. I knew people got married, had kids and that was the end. Honestly, I don't even remember when I realized what sex was but what I am trying to say is that we never swore in front of elders, we never fought in public and we certainly never spoke about inappropriate things.

Times have changed, kids.

If the parents out there are wondering how kids were so well behaved, I will amount it to the few spankings I got when I was a kid and that look from my mom. You know the one I am talking about...when you start making a scene at the store and you know you are about to get an ass whoopin when you get home.

I don't know if the Brown family was always the way they behaved when we arrived, but they were certainly far from "an honorable family" as my grandmother would say.

We only stayed with them for about three days and the space was tight. It was one of those weird houses that appeared large and structured on the outside, but once you went inside, you saw all the small spaces and strange nooks everywhere...it made me feel claustrophobic. To make it worse, it was super dark – the décor, the paint, the lighting.

I don't like dark. I am one of those girls who turns on every light in the house.

Again, we've been over this – I don't scare easy, and for those who do turn on the lights because they are scared, do you really think if someone was in your house to kill you, they would just walk away because you turned the lights on?

I just like bright places – the more windows, the better.

Anyway, back to the Brown family.

Their house and behavior would give any Albanian grandmother an instant heart attack.

The house was messy and uncleaned. *God forbid.*

When Mrs. Brown would get ready in the morning, she would walk around the house in a bra and no shirt. *I think I just heard all the grandmas' fainting in the distance.*

One day, Mrs. Brown's daughter yelled, "Fuck you!" because her mother would not let her go out with her friends. *Hell, to the no.*

On our last day there, Mr. Brown threw rubber flip flops at his son to get him to wake up and clean the house. *That shit was actually pretty funny.*

I might be sounding ungrateful and judgmental to you because hey, at least they were willing to help us, right? The story is not over kids.

The land of the free is not free. It's expensive. So, along with everything else – uprooting your whole life – it was also expected that you brought money with you from Albania. Just some cushion money to get started. Seems reasonable enough and my parents had great jobs in Albania. My dad was a personal driver to an oil tycoon – oil was a big deal in Albania. I'm surprised the US has not invaded yet... but, he was not just a driver. He was a driver and a body guard and he needed to know how to drive, creatively, at night.

No, it was not because his boss was a philandering man – it was because business was risky and people didn't play by the law. My mom was an HR director for the largest natural gas company in Fier. You can say my family dabbled in just about everything – we had police officers, drivers, HR directors, senators, border patrol, etc.

It was great money in Albania, but have you looked at the conversion rate recently? It wasn't so great back then either.

$17,000. That was the amount we had when we arrived to the States.

You're surprised I told you?

I told you for three reasons:

1. Honesty

2. Story telling purposes.

3. Reality

As you can remember, there are only a few things that irk me. When people say, oh yeah, I came to the States with $10 in my pocket – they are not only lying, but they are delusional. I was watching something recently in which a guy was like, "I had seven dollars in my pocket when I came to the States and now I own four restaurants."

Hold the fuck up.

Yes, maybe you did have $7 in your pocket, but where was the rest? Who paid for your plane ticket? Where did you live with $7? What did you eat? Did you just hop of the fucking plane and walk into a job? Oh! If you had kids when you moved, there is absolutely no way you only had that much money.

Now, I understand sacrifice – trust me, but some things just don't need to be over played for sensitive reasons.

The part about this whole thing that irks me the most is that they jump. They go from having nothing to having everything.

You want to know what a breath of fresh air is?

The story of how you got there. The struggle, because everybody can relate to that and maybe see the light at the end of the long tunnel. You're not Harry Potter. You didn't just wave your fucking wand and magically you had everything you wanted. That shit takes a LOT of hard work and sacrifices.

Okay, rant over.

The ever-magnificent Brown family (can you hear the sarcasm in my voice?) showed us the ropes. After we moved to our cupboard sized house, registered to our schools, and my parents got jobs at the local factory, they took us to all the stores. We bought groceries, a car, mattresses, and a bedroom set for my parents. We paid all the house bills, and first and last for rent. You see all this money that you need? I don't think $7 can cover it.

Still don't see a problem? I'll tell you.

Remember the Brown family had been here a while so they would know what was really necessary to just get started. Well, apparently, they had selective memory.

Let me tell you. You don't need a crappy "new" car which would die in less than two years. You don't need a tacky bedroom set, complete with a dresser and head board. You don't need expensive ass walnuts from Costco. You don't need new everything.

What do you actually do?

You buy a used car. You take as many free things as other Albanians will give you. You buy mattresses, but no bedroom set. You buy only the necessities when it comes to food at the cheapest store you can find. You sacrifice – that way, you can live a little better and then a little better – until you can afford the life you want.

That day I was told to go back where I came from, I went home to find out that my parents had silently been hyperventilating for the past two weeks because our rent was due at the end of the week, and their paychecks had not arrived in the mail yet. Our rent was only $800 at the time – not too shabby, but our available balance at the time?

$8.30

If you have ever faced eviction, you know what I mean when I say the air outside suddenly becomes colder at the thought that you might not have a roof over your head in a few days. I might not have understood a lot when I was eight, but that was crystal clear.

My dad was too prideful to ask his family for help. He would wait it out until the very end before he had to ask. He was the eldest – he was supposed to take care of them and he was supposed to sell the beautiful hope of America, not the heartbreaking reality. Every time they called, you know what he said?

We're fine. It's great here.

Oh, I almost forgot. The Brown family.

They would not answer their phone and my parents called - often. They never took our money, or stole from us, but then again, some people want to watch the world burn and some people want to burn down others to make themselves feel better.

The check came on time, by the way. We stayed in that house for three years before we moved to a bigger house, but after that split-second money panic – everything was tight.

I remember when my mom was learning how to drive, we would also go furniture hunting. It was a game my parents would play – I guess to distract us from the tight situation we were in. We didn't have money to afford anything new for a while, so as my mom would slowly drive around the neighborhood – right around midnight – my sister and I would compete to spot a piece of furniture someone had put out on the street for us to take home.

You are thinking one of the two following things:

That's disgusting.

That's so fucking sad.

Well, we made sure to deep clean anything we picked up, we never took things like a mattress, and I didn't really think about it. You can't think something is bad if you have nothing to compare it to. Sure, later on – like right now, I realize it was sad as fuck and it did suck. I don't think any kid wants to pick up furniture on the street, but hey, remember this isn't a movie, and to me the roughest parts haven't even really happened yet, because the only time something can really hurt is when you know what pain feels like, and you are clearly conscious that you are right in the middle of it.

Besides, sometimes it was funny.

A few months ago, my dad told me about this family that had just immigrated to the US and they were driving around trying to find some used furniture like we used to. Well, a white American family was unloading their new furniture and you guessed it. They left a brand-new couch on the sidewalk as they figured out the rest. The Albanian family took it thinking it was out with the trash.

I am literally laughing out loud right now. You don't think it's funny? Oh well.

Lesson of the Chapter

The only way out is through.

CHAPTER 10

Maria! How Could You!?

Yⁿou see that woman sitting there, on her typewriter? Her soft curly hair is cascading down around her face and her brown eyes are relentlessly focusing on the keys of the typewriter. Her face is small and round, but her nose is long and pointed. There is a sparkle in her eyes – a youthfulness. She is content, calm – like her life is going exactly how everybody expected.

We will get to her soon. First, a topic everybody just loves.

Middle school.

Did you just shutter at those words? Well, I sort of did too.

It was not actually that bad for me. I know, you're shocked. It wasn't a great time either, but nothing necessarily jumps out at me. The usual going through puberty embarrassment which I am pretty sure I have shoved into a corner of my memory that I don't remember. I remember more of what happened when I wasn't at school.

I do remember this one time I was in homeroom and this kid freaked out. I think he asked the teacher to go to the bathroom or the library and for some reason the teacher said no – he was sort of moody. The kid grabbed the small lamp on the teacher's desk and threw it at him. It missed the teacher's head – instead it smashed on the blackboard behind him. I know it's not funny, but it was the most shocking thing to happen in our small town middle school.

I don't know how your middle school was structured, but in the seventh grade we got to start foreign languages. We had to take half a year of Spanish and half a year of French, so that we could make a calculated decision when arriving to the 8th grade and then high school. When the time came to make a decision, literally, everybody chose Spanish because it was easy. Before you start throwing tomatoes or curse words at me, I am not saying knowing how to speak Spanish is easy or offending the language – I am just stating facts.

Take it from someone who ended up taking French for seven years, nobody wants to sit through French grammar lessons. I only thought English was a hard language until I learned French conditional sentences. Honestly, the only reason I stuck with it in high school was because it would look great on my college application and the teacher was a British cutie. He actually taught French and Italian – our school system was seriously lacking funding.

Anyway, remember how I remember more of what happen outside of middle school? It was probably a mental suppression tactic, but I remember spending a lot of time with my sister.

After the first factory job my parents had – they both moved on to separate jobs. My dad got a job at a garage for a major bus line. He mostly changed tires, but sometimes he would get to use his mechanic skills. My mom started working at a hotel as a house keeper and as a bagger at a grocery store. My sister and I are four years apart, so we never went to the same school at the same time.

How did we spend so much time together?

My mom worked at the hotel from 7AM until 5PM. Then, she went to the super market job from 6PM until 11PM. She would take the bus to the hotel. Then she would get back on it to get to the super market, but when she got out of work at 11PM there was no bus that she could take.

My dad worked at the bus line from 3PM until 11PM. He drove to and from work – an hour each way.

My sister and I went to school and when we went home there was nobody there. We did our homework, made dinner and watched TV. Why were we so well behaved?

Immigrant Child Syndrome.

You never want to disappoint your parents. Ask any immigrant or foreign born citizen – disappointment is worse than when your parents yell at you.

The only thing we didn't really do was sleep. I mean, we weren't vampires, but we didn't necessarily have a curfew. Maybe that's when I built up my system to be able to function with four to five hours of sleep. The reason we didn't sleep before, at least 11:45PM each night is because we would wait for our mom to come home. She didn't ask us to, but it was habit.

We had to fill our time with something after dinner and homework so like any child out there, we turned to the TV. Clearly, paying for any sort of cable other than the most basic, was out of the question so our choices were limited. The news was always depressing. We had no interest in seemingly weird American shows. Game shows were odd. The only choice left was Univision.

If you don't know what the Univision channel is, you should check it out. It's a Spanish network – actually the most prominent and influential one, and at the time it had an array of telenovelas (soap operas). They were dramatic. They were over the top. They were completely unrealistic. They were our favorite. It was part of the reason I didn't take Spanish in high school, and I actually think I got my flare for dramatic plots and writing style from them.

Remember when I told you kids soak up new things because there isn't as much on their mind – so much stressing and worrying them. Well, here's your proof.

I watched Spanish telenovelas every single night, and without ever hearing the Spanish language before or even knowing it existed, I learned it. I picked it up quick and to this day I can translate Spanish perfectly. I can hold a conversation and get around in a Spanish speaking country, but Spanish is not my first language…which speaking of that, let me tell you about something that really *irks* me.

I don't walk around telling everybody I speak three languages because that's just douche like behavior, but when it naturally comes up in conversation I join in. Perfect example – in college, a group of my friend's friends were talking about the new album a reggaeton artist, I happen to listen to, had released.

Don't look at me like that.

Yes, I listen to reggaeton and yes, I get weird looks from people when I'm in the car, but music is the best way to never forget a language you have learned. AND, I don't only listen to reggaeton – there is a song for almost everything in Spanish. When you are sad, when you are crushing on someone, when an ex comes back into your life, when you want to let the inner gangster in you out, when you want to dance, when you want to be sweetly romantic, when you are trying to get some writing done (like right now), when you want to work out, and especially when you want to let your freak flag fly.

Regardless, this girl, in the group of "friends", didn't believe me when I said I listen to the artist because there was no way some white girl from Albania knew Spanish. She asked me to say car in Spanish.

Really? Okay.

I answered, as politely as I could, and she tells me, "It's not carro, it's coche."

That might be so, but you are still a bitch.

That's what irks me. It's wasn't the side eye and it wasn't the predetermined image she had of me – it was her attitude, because if someone came up to me and told me they spoke Albanian, do you know what I would say?

That's amazing! Because Albanian is a fucking difficult language to learn.

Back to my point. I never took a single lesson of Spanish before I learned it, and I took French for SEVEN years. Do you want to take a bet as to which I feel more comfortable speaking?

Yep, Spanish. I learned Spanish as a kid and French as a teen. Point proven.

Oh, what's that? You don't believe me?

Well, then you explain to me why I speak perfect English and after 17 years in America, my parents still need help with translating mail, doctor's notes and work forms. I love them even more for it, by the way. Their broken English is a sign of bravery which most people would never have.

After our nightly routine of homework, dinner, and telenovelas, my sister and I would go outside. We had a fairly large balcony type area – it was probably as large as the damn roof, we called our home, but regardless, my sister and I would sit on the floor by the railing, overlooking the driveway at 11:35PM, every night, and wait for our mom to come home.

She walked home.

1.8 miles.

45 minutes.

Every night.

Rain.

Snow.

-10 degree weather.

Monday through Friday.

She never came home empty handed either. She always carried home groceries or a snack for us.

In Albania, women didn't drive. It wasn't illegal, but it might as well have been. The men had the better paying jobs – sounds like a story every woman has heard before – and if a woman drove it was automatically assumed that she was a slut. She was sleeping around and her lover was paying for the car because she couldn't afford to, and there was no husband out there paying for a woman to be independent.

Gotta love the good old days.

Obviously, my mom didn't know how to drive when we got to the States and there was no point in learning right away. Why?

The fucking Brown family.

We didn't have enough money for my mom to even get a license let alone a car. So, she had two jobs and no car for the first year. When she wasn't walking from work, she was walking to get groceries. All three of us did.

My mom, my sister and I would walk about two to three miles from our house to the closest grocery store and then we would walk back home with grocery bags in hand. I guess that's the sucky part about a small, suburban town – no bus or public transport.

You see the woman sitting there, on the edge of the bed?

She's the same one from the beginning of the chapter, except for 17 years have passed.

Her hair is in a bun on top of her head. Her face is tired and her body is relaxed – preparing for bed. She licks her dry lips and feels the four pills in her hand; one to control the blood sugar levels, one to ease the pain, one for her high blood pressure, and one to rebuild the fluid missing in her knees.

She's my mom.

Lesson of the Chapter

Sacrifice can instill a deep, deep guilt in a person's heart.

CHAPTER 11

Merry Christmas. Happy Ramadan

I love Rizzoli & Isles.

It's a TV show on TNT – well actually *was* a TV show. They aired their last season in the fall of 2016. If you don't know it – it was a crime/cop type of show, but unlike everything else out there, it was not in New York or Chicago. It was in Boston. I mean really how many shows does Chicago need? Chicago PD, Chicago Fire, Chicago Med, Chicago Justice. Like, damn, we get it – Chicago has the most attractive doctors, cops, detectives, and legal prosecutors.

Anyway, Rizzoli & Isles was also one of those shows that just focused on a total of six or seven characters and developed their lives over seven seasons. Besides the fact that it was in Boston, I loved it for two reasons.

One; the two main characters were women in male dominated fields – a detective and a chief medical examiner. Which also, by the way, focused on their work, family and friends and not on finding their husband or love interest. Yes, there were romances through the seasons, but they did not heavily focus on them, and they were realistic.

Second; one of the two main characters – the detective – reminds me of myself, not only because she was fucking Amazonian in height, but also because she could take care of herself. She had two brothers, but when a criminal was after her, she could whip out her own damn gun and defend herself.

Anyway, a reoccurring theme in the show was a serial killer they dealt with. I remember one time they made a psychological connection as to why he was the way he was. Usually, it has a lot to do with their childhood – obviously, but they mentioned religion. Not a specific religion, but more the parents' different religions and the fact that they let him chose which he wanted to be. They claim it lead to his confusion and lack of identity – lack of structure while he was growing up. Now, I did not turn out a serial killer, but in the religious section – there was a shit ton of confusion and lack of structure for me.

I know. Some of you might skip this chapter. Religion tends to be one of those subjects nobody wants to discuss. I feel like for some people it's almost as bad as when your parents start to talk about sex, but ya'll need to chill. It's not that bad.

Remember those warnings I gave you in the beginning…. specifically, #2?

Well, you might definitely not like my opinions in this chapter, but stop for a second and look around. Is anybody forcing you to read this? Nope. Walk away if you have to.

My mom's side is Orthodox. No, we didn't go to church every Sunday. No, we don't participate in Lent. Yes, we celebrate Christmas. Yes, we celebrate Easter. No, we don't confirm kid's in church. *AND*, no, I was not baptized.

My dad's side is Muslim. Yes, they celebrate Ramadan. No, they don't go to the mosque. Yes, they eat pork. No, they don't fast for Ramadan.

If you are still reading this, you are probably thinking *what the fuck? None of these things make sense for those religions.* The traditional way you are used to thinking about religion is not what I had.

Let me tell you why.

Remember the history lesson about Albania?

My dad's family was one of the many, many people who converter when the Ottoman Empire took over, and my mom's family remained Orthodox. Back then, religion was a lot more serious – a lot more practiced and I am sure in numerous countries it still is. It would have remained a major influence in Albania too, but Hoxha didn't think religion was very patriotic. He thought it caused unnecessary tension and distraction. The only God anybody needed, according to him, was the government.

So, when he took over, he closed all the churches and mosques in Albania and declared the nation atheist. After centuries of religion, of belief, of faith – the Albanian people weren't supposed to believe in anything they knew except the government.

44 years of no imagination.

That why this chapter is important in my life.

Imagination. Why do I say that? Because to me, that's what religion is. You have blind faith in something that doesn't exist – something that is unobtainable, untouchable.

From Albania, With Love

Now, that I think about it.... every writer has their own religion. Not a group of people following and believing, but they have created something that does not exist, something you cannot touch, people that aren't real, and worlds that make other people feel like they aren't alone.

If other artists out there are offended – I don't care. I respect your work immensely, but I can hear a song, I can touch a painting, I can watch a movie, but I can't see characters – they live only in my imagination.

Okay, back to atheist Albania.

The Albanian people may be a lot of things, but here's a sure thing – we are no fucking quitters.

Even under Hoxha's rule, we still celebrated. I remember my grandma telling me that they had a small radio in the kitchen during that time. When Easter rolled around, they dyed eggs and no, we didn't do some Easter bunny shit – they were painted red; the color of blood. We dye them on Thursday when Jesus, allegedly, was killed and we celebrate on Sunday when Jesus hopped up and basically said, "Surprise, bitches! I'm back."

We usually dye boiled eggs for each member of the family and then, on Sunday, we crack the eggs, taking turns – whoever has the egg that doesn't crack, wins, and has luck the rest of the year.

At the time, the problem was this whole declared atheist bullshit. People passed the red dye around in secret. When Sunday came, my grandma told me, they gathered in the kitchen and turned off all the other lights in the house as if they were sleeping. They did a little celebration with the eggs and ate some delicious yshmer (*look it up*) as quietly as they could.

Why?

Such celebrations were illegal, so the little radio in the kitchen was a secret device everybody in the neighborhood had. When someone heard the secret police patrolling the streets, they would radio and tell everybody else to not make any noise as not to get caught and put in front of a firing squad.

Are you surprised that you don't know a country in Europe lived in such restricted and oppressed times on the brink of the 21st century?

Well, that's what happens when history books don't give a shit to include you, and Hollywood continues to run with their stereotypical agenda.

Two things happened as a result of this religious oppression; one good, one bad. It can never be all good.

The great thing was that, after Hoxha, people understood each other – they understood the other side. They had been through this time together. They had both been oppressed – forced to hide their faith and celebrate in secret. There was no animosity among these strikingly different religions. Both sides respected each other and allowed for room to practice their faith without judgement.

There was room for flexibility and there was hope for new ideas. Religion became a sort of symbol of resistance rather than a perfectly practiced faith for both sides.

From Albania, With Love

The bad thing to come out of this difficult time was a social norm. Hoxha forbid religion because he wanted people to be nationalists – he wanted them to believe in something tangible; something you could see, and work for. A sort of status.

Now, some people didn't mind him and his ideals. I have plenty of family members who thought his time was the best as everybody was taken care off and I don't really care, but the one thing they took from his ideals was the sense of security. I think you know where I am going with this. Certain jobs were seen as secure and honorable. Others, were simply seen as dreamers that had lost their mind and would never financially support themselves. They were slackers, lazy, and crazy.

All the immigrant children out there reading this will know exactly what I am talking about. Your dad, your grandpa, your aunts and uncles will be oh so proud of you if you work in an office, if you become a doctor, if you become a lawyer, if you become an architect, if you become a scientist, and especially if you go anywhere in the business world.

If you want to give your immigrant family a heart attack – tell them you want an art degree, tell them you want to be a writer, tell them you want to be a singer, tell them you want to be an English major.

You get my point and please remember it as this is not even the tip of the iceberg.

Anyways, back to religion.

I don't think I need to remind you, but I lived with my grandparents on my mom's side…technically my grandma more than anybody else. So, I was raised with Christmas and Easter. My parents never sat me down and said here are your options on religion, because it was never that deep. It did not make a person's identity – it did not make them who they were. Sure, it might sway their decisions or life path, but what you have faith in has nothing to do with who you end up becoming.

I know a few of you might not agree with me because of this example and that example, but I don't mind. You are entitled to your opinion, but from what I have seen, been through and discovered – your choices are always your own. You'll see.

I've never had a favorite holiday. In Albania, presents were handed out on New Year's. We didn't have Santa – we had the old man of New Year's, but still New Year's was not my favorite holiday even as a kid who wanted toys.

Instead, I had a favorite week. December 24th – December 31st.

On the morning on December 24th, my grandma and I would get up at 5AM and lay sheets all over the house. On the floor, on the couch, on the beds – everywhere but the bathroom. Then we would go into the kitchen and I would sit on a chair, with my knees pulled up and watch my grandma knead the dough.

From Albania, With Love

Have you ever tried baklava? Well, if you haven't I highly suggest it. There are a billion different recipes for it, but we made it with four ingredients only; olive oil, a shit ton of sugar, walnuts, and filo dough. Filo dough – if you have never handled it – is a thin, thin layer of dough. It's thinner than printing paper and you need about 50 sheets to make one large baklava.

On Christmas eve morning, my grandma rolled out every single sheet by hand and I laid them out on the sheets spread around the house. Then we prepped the stuffing; walnuts and a shit ton of sugar. The doors where propped open, the smell of sugar was in the air, and there was a huge smile on my face – every year. It was pure bliss and it was the best start to my favorite week of the year.

The rest of the week, you ask?

It was spent with family, food and talking – lots of talking. Distant cousins, uncles, aunts, parents, grandparents, and neighbors on both sides of the family. We all got together at my grandma's house on New Year's Eve and at midnight, we set of fireworks to welcome the New Year. We were all there – all 50 plus family members, wishing each other a happy and healthy new year. Muslim. Orthodox. Atheists. It didn't matter to me or anybody else. To others, religion might be a church or a mosque, or a temple, but I don't feel I needed any of those things.

Go ahead and tell me that's why I have a foul mouth, or no structure or why I am currently unemployed, because I don't care. Not having those sort of restrictions, worries about where I was going to go after drawing my last breath, or trying so hard to fit into a box has helped me understand people so much more. Most importantly, it has helped me understand faith in myself on a level unimaginable. If you strip away everything that you think makes up a person, do you know what's left?

A human soul.

That's my religion.

Lesson of the Chapter

Faith is persistence pushing imagination forward.

From Albania, With Love

CHAPTER 12

Through The Window, Through The Wall

When a family immigrates to the United States, the first vacation they take, after they are settled – is back to their home country. Ask anybody. It's a big affair and now that I'm thinking back to it – it's far from my favorite thing.

Don't get me wrong. I love travelling. I am one of those weird people. I am not afraid of planes or flying. I actually get thrilled when I book a flight somewhere – maybe I'm excited to go somewhere new or maybe I am excited to leave my everyday life for just a little bit. Even still, I love the aspect of discovering a new place. I don't necessarily enjoy living out of a suitcase, but I can make it work, especially when a beautiful new place is waiting for me.

Lately the only trips I've been taking have been to get coffee. You know, being unemployed doesn't really help in the whole disposable income department.

When I was a sophomore in college I went to China and Hong Kong. There was a program they offered – it wasn't much of an offer as you paid $3,500 for it and it was technically required for my International Business degree, but an experience non-the less. It was structured into a two-week class during Winter Break and it was wonderful – a story for later.

Though let me tell you, the flight there was excruciating. We flew from Boston to Detroit – the easiest leg of the trip. Then, from Detroit, we flew to Beijing.

14 hours.

840 fucking minutes.

I read three books, and not little bitch books either – they were about 350 pages each. I walked around as not to get a clot. I tried to ignore my annoying friend sitting three seats in front of me, and then when we landed I just wanted to pass out. It was weird though – I am still fascinated with how a plane can get you to a completely different world, 6,622 miles away, in just over half a day.

The flight back was even worse. Hong Kong to Detroit.

17 hours.

And, yours truly, over here, had bronchitis while also sitting next to the most aggravating classmate who kept leaning forward to check on her boyfriend, because he was scared to fly. That's exactly what a pretend macho guy needs – someone holding his hand and constantly asking if he's okay. Clearly, he's not okay. He's pale as fuck and he's not going anywhere soon. We are all trapped up here with recycled air – 40,000 feet above the ground.

Ohh, hold up…I forgot. Even better. He was not actually her boyfriend unless you consider having shower sex a relationship.

The walls were thin in the hotels of China, kids, but hey, you do you girl!

From Albania, With Love

Anyway, like I was saying – I could do without the 17 hour flights in economy, but I don't mind travelling.

I was ten years old when we planned our first vacation back to Albania. I was excited to see my family. I was excited to see my grandma. I especially was excited to go to the beach.

Albania has the best beaches and they have a variety too. Sandy. Rocky. Deep. Shallow. No matter what sort of beach though, every single one is beautifully clear and still. You could always see your feet at the bottom of the sea floor.

As I mentioned, the first trip back home is monumental. It's your chance to show everybody how great America is, how well we are doing, how advanced my sister and I are in school, what great jobs my parents have, and how happy we are.

I know what you're thinking…but did we actually have any of those things?

The simple answer is no; however, you remember those people watching us from the balcony as we were leaving, and the over played image the US has in other countries?

It's not that people don't want to be honest – it's that they are too proud to say the truth. Too proud to say they cried because it's difficult, too proud to say they have bad jobs because they had the best in their country, and too proud to not use their kids to show off because their kids are a product of them after all.

So, how could we show them that we were living the best life possible?

Money.

Or should I say – gifts… for every single member of the family.

Cut to the few months before we headed back to Albania after being in the US for two years. My parents had worked their asses off at jobs they did not necessarily enjoy. I never saw my dad as he went to work when I came from school and by the time he got home, I was already in bed. I only saw my mom for about 30 minutes a day – if you combine the morning and before I went to bed each night. As I told you, after the money/rent scare we had, things were tight, but working three jobs between my parents helped us accumulate some savings.

Savings we should have been smarter with. Savings we should have used for education or something useful.

Do you know where most of the money went?

You guessed it. To our "vacation". Between paying our rent, our bills, our flights, our extra suitcases, and buying gifts for everybody and their mother – our savings were basically cleared out.

$10,000.

I just lost my mind for the thousandth time as I remember that that's how much we spent for our vacation, for our family, for a lie.

Ohh… the best part of it all was that our family didn't say thank you once because it was our duty.

Anybody else would have lost their shit with the amount of times our family claimed it was our duty to support them. Why was it our duty? Well, we were in the oh so perfect United States of America. What could we possibly have to complain about?

By the time my parents bought the house they have now, they also got their passports. For any of you out there that don't know how it works, here you go;

After five years of working in the US, paying taxes, and just being a good citizen – they allow you to apply to become a citizen. At the interview, they ask you difficult ass questions, that not even high schoolers can answer, and if you pass you become a citizen.

Under our Constitution, some powers belong to the states. What is one power of the states?

What happened at the Constitutional Convention?

The House of Representatives has how many voting members?

It may seem simple to some of you out there, but not so much for foreign born people who lived in a government that closed its self from the rest of the world.

My parents studied for months and they passed on their first try.

You know how it was our duty to take care of the family? Well, after my parents got their passport and new house, they were also expected to host the family who wanted to visit us as many times as they pleased.

107

Migena Dulaj

My sister's appeasing behavior faded quick and the second time my father's parents visited, they stayed with an aunt of mine, who came to the US with the lottery about six or seven years after us. She will reappear again so let's call her Aunt Beatrice. She was also the one who was friends with the Brown family, by the way, so you can imagine how much I like her.

My dad was still not over the whole eldest child syndrome – I guess, so he gave his father my house key, because my grandfather liked to walk. We live about two miles away from aunt Beatrice. I didn't know he had taken my key and apparently, people can just enter our house as they please.

AND, don't look at me like that. I'm well aware he's my grandfather, but I think you know me pretty well by now to know that I like my independence and liberty. He wants to enter the house – he can fucking knock on the front door.

I came home one day after school and realized I didn't have a key. Nobody was coming home until after six – it was 2:30PM. I took mostly advanced placement courses in high school so you can imagine my work load. I am very patient, and I know people who aren't say that, but I really am – you'll see. I, however, don't like waiting when I can do something.

I grabbed the ladder in the garage and I wiggled open a window I knew was loose. I rolled into the house like I was casing the place because I had to respect my elders and give them my keys to maybe – potentially use on a house that was not even theirs. Do I sound bitter?

I'm not and maybe this isn't the most honorable and Albanian thing to say, but I don't respect my elders – even my family – unless they respect me. You gotta give to get. I will never be rude, but better believe the whole bloodline bullshit my father tried to feed me when I was younger certainly did not stick.

I know some of this may not make sense to you and you may think I'm being a bitch, but remember when I told you this was my story?

It is and yes, a *LOT* more real shit happened in our family, but I don't really think about it too much. It shaped me to be whoever I was supposed to be for that moment, and it did contribute to my internalizing method, but now I've come to realize much more important things.

I'll explain – I promise – it's the whole point of this long journey.

Do I still talk to my extended family? *Not really.*
Is that vague? *Yes.*

Do I regret how I handled some situations? *Nope.*

There are *MANY, MANY* reasons, ideals, and situations which lead me to listen to myself and ask myself if my family was a real reflection of how I felt about something or what I believed in, or who I wanted to become. It's the hardest thing someone can do – distance themselves from their family and make up their own mind because it's socially not accepted, it's a shame, it's not right, and many believe you are who you are due to your family, but I don't believe in that.

You'll see in a bit, but I have realized that if you take the most extreme situation – death, people will blame you for the decisions you took and who you were. Not once will they say your actions were due to who your family was, so you might as well live your life and take decisions which reflect you and who you are, not your family.

For me, while yes, there were some actions my family took which I did not agree with, it was mostly their ideals that lead me to reflect on who I was becoming and what I believed in. While I don't remember every detail of my childhood or my family's perspective on certain things, some moments remain with me.

My family always had this thing about birthdays. They would always make a big deal and when we were in Albania, we would always get together. They liked celebrating happy times – I mean, who doesn't?

One time, we were at a party for someone's birthday and I remember my mom asking one of her sisters about some friend she had that my mom had not seen in a while.

My aunt didn't talk to the friend anymore.

They had found the friend on the roof of her apartment building right before she attempted to commit suicide.

"She has lost her mind and she needs to go find it."

That's how my aunt described her friend's mental state, and the rest of my family wasn't too far behind in agreeing with her.

Lesson of the Chapter

Family is not a definition of who you are.

CHAPTER 13

Burek, Pite & Everything Else That Gave Me An Ass

I went to a pretty small university in Rhode Island. It has a stellar International Business program and your usual collection of college kids. There were only about 800 or so kids in my graduating class, but every senior looked forward to the living arrangements. You see, senior year we got to live in townhouses. They were split up by neighborhoods or blocks. Their sized depended on how many people you wanted to live with, but it could go up to eight. Those were usually reserved for the sparse Greek frats and sororities we had on campus.

I lived in a five-people town house. We had a kitchen, living room, bathroom and single room downstairs. Upstairs there was a bathroom, two single bedrooms and one double. I don't like the first floor of anything – it brings back a bad memory from childhood (*a story for another time*) and there was no way I was sharing.

Why?

When you go to a small university you run the chance that the group of friends or people you are willing to live with is limited and established since Freshman year.

Remember Naira?

The one I saved from that football player freshman year?

Well, even though now we are totally fine – back then she went totally ballistic on me. She was one of the first friends I made in college and I thought we got along great until our friendship turned into nothing but talking about other people, her always being the center of attention, and when it came time to pick roommates Sophomore year – I took one for the team and agreed to be her roommate because nobody else in the group wanted. I didn't mind because it seemed like my sister had passed along the appeasing characteristic to me, but I had it in a sort of not caring way. I just don't like fighting. Don't take me for weak though – if I need to fight, I will, but I would prefer to just mind my own damn business.

Side Bar.

A word of advice to you girls out there. If you have a friend that constantly talks about others when she is with you, chances are, she is talking shit about you when you aren't there.

The main reason why Naira and I ended our friendship is because she was all or nothing. I know I said I am like that in a friendship as well, but I meant in the supporting you department, not in the let's hang out every single day and be attached at the hip sort of thing. I need my space – I just can't. It got to a point when mutual friends would ask me where she was when they saw me alone. No. I don't roll like that. I am my own person and she is her own person.

I guess they say everybody comes into your life for a reason and maybe her point was to show me my independence on a new level. It took about two years for us to be cool by the way – since mid-sophomore year until beginning of senior year it was daggers out of her eyes every time she saw me. It didn't help that we were part of a lot of the same on campus organizations. One of our favorite advisors, who cared about us both, had a sit down with us before Columbus Day weekend. It was useless. Naira somehow managed to weave in her grandmother and then she started crying.

Pause.

General census; if a girl starts crying during an argument it means she knows she's wrong and is now playing the sad/pity card so you will feel bad.

My census; If I ever start crying during an argument it is probably because I am so mad at the situation and then I will cry because I'm angry that I'm even crying about it.

The "resolution" meeting was useless, by the way. I was over it. I didn't even want to fight anymore. I let her cry, even though if she wanted to play the grandparent card, I could have played the dead grandfather card, or the "my grandma is 4,000 miles away" card, but like I said, I just wanted to go home for the long weekend. She was being childish and when I realize that, I shutdown.

After we parted ways, she started rumors about me and told people I throw myself on guys. I am laughing right now as I am writing this.

From Albania, With Love

Here's another fact about me. I don't give a flying fuck what people say about me. Rumors hold no space in my reality and if she thought saying I was a hoe would do any damage, she was more childish than I thought. Some girls would be worried that guys might not want to approach after hearing rumors like that, but here's how I see it. If a guy doesn't have the balls to approach me just because of a rumor, he can be on his merry way – away from me.

I didn't start rumors about her or do anything. I figured she was hurt and she needed to figure herself out.

Anyway, when senior year came around, I was still living with some of the girls I had been with sophomore and junior year, so I made it known that I fucking deserved a single for putting up with Naira. I got the single upstairs.

Our house was in a prime location – a little distant from the other blocks and when it came to parties, the house was almost sound proof. The best thing about living in the town houses, to me, was that when you didn't feel like getting dolled up and really putting in an effort to go to a party, you could go down to the popular sections in your sweatpants and just watch the under classmen do the most.

One night, me and the housemate who had the single down stairs, got dressed in our sweats, sans makeup, and went down to see all the craziness of a Friday night.

This specific house mate will reappear later for other purposes so let's call her Marina.

You know when you are a senior, in high school or college, and you walk around campus sort of like you own the place. It's an attitude thing – you're the oldest, the most powerful now. That's the attitude Marina and I had as we walked down to the other townhouses. We both wore all black; black sweater and black sweatpants. Coincidently enough that's also what the resident advisors wore. They could write people up – basically get them in trouble, especially if there was underage drinking.

On our way down, towards the noise, I noticed a group of three girls. They were freshman for sure – I could tell by the nervous look in their eyes and their twitching hands, AND they were dressed to the nines – something upperclassmen didn't bother with on a random Friday. As we got closer to them, I noticed they looked up and their eyes grew about two sizes as they quickly dumped their drinks in the bushes next to them.

They thought we were resident advisors. I played along, because it's fun.

The point of the story?

People will believe whatever you want them to think you are. Attitude is everything. What you think you are, you will project.

Those girls believed we were RAs because of the way we were walking, because of our self-assurance and dominance. Nowhere did we have the RA symbol on our clothing or badges hanging from our necks.

Why is this important?

From Albania, With Love

Body image issues. (*I can almost hear all the boys skipping pages to the next chapter, but who gives a fuck – let's continues.*)

In Albania, believe it or not, when I was younger, I never felt bad about my body or my weight. I lived around the sort of grandma who constantly force fed me and complained that I was too skinny. And, she was right.

When I arrived to the US, I was stick thin – like someone could run through my thighs without ever touching me type of thin. The problem was with American food. The portions are out of control and I was not really careful. I will take full responsibility for that, but best believe I don't feel bad for my body or the way I look.

You see, there is a clear difference between healthy and unhealthy.

Apparently, my family forgot this tiny fact.

That wonderful vacation we took back to Albania, when I was 10 – it was filled with sideways comments about my weight. I grew very fast – remember that I'm Amazonian – so my height was a lot of what they were seeing. Believe me when I say, I was still thin and I was still a child. For some reason, it never really bothered me. No, I was not about to walk around naked, but I didn't think it mattered much.

I didn't start really gaining weight until I got to high school, but I played volleyball all four years so I was getting exercise. It still didn't stop my family from commenting though. Every holiday, every family gathering – it was like they thought they were doing me a favor of some sort, helping me out, because maybe I didn't know any better.

Our family had gathered for Thanksgiving one year – I think it was about eight or nine years ago and Aunt Beatrice came up to me as I was setting the table.

"You know, I have heard of this new diet. I think you should try it."

Oh great, here we go.

"You put the food in your mouth and you chew to get the flavor, but then you don't swallow so that you don't gain any weight."

I swear, I can't make this shit up.

That was my family's Thanksgiving. My aunt basically suggesting I become anorexic...I don't really know which category to even put that "diet" into.

So, why do I freely walk around the house with no pants on, even if I don't have a society perfect body?

Firstly, because fuck society standards.

Secondly, we get back to the immigrant child syndrome.

A side effect of the syndrome is thick skin. Remember kids would tell me to go back to where I came from and call me a million other hurtful, stereotypical names?

Well, one can either cower or let their words bounce of your chest like you're wearing a shield, because you realize that they might be hurt, or misguided or scared about something they don't understand. I chose the second route and only listened to myself. Not that it was easy.

From Albania, With Love

It doesn't help to see thin girls on book covers, in movies, as popular singers and of course my all-time favorite; Victoria's Secret models. I have nothing against them – all the power to them. My problem stems from the fact that young girls think they have to look like that. Do you know why those models look like that? No, I was not going to say plastic surgery. It's because it's their job. Literally it's in their contract that they have to look like that. They wake up and go to the gym because it's their job.

The worst problem of this whole thing, to me, is that girls want to look like that for someone else. Usually guys, because media tells them that's what guys want and that's what people find attractive. Well, fuck that, because guess what?

Healthy beats out "cultivated/photo shopped attractive for five minutes" any day.

Healthy does not have a size, a number, a weight, a model look. Someone could weigh 170 pounds and look rounder or thinner or stronger than someone else who weighs the same.

Just because someone weighs less than me, doesn't mean they can outrun me or climb the stairs faster than me.

That's health – your body being in balance and strong.

AND, if there are guys or even family members in your life who tell you to lose weight or tell you, you look fat or tell you your body is not attractive.... you can tell them to fuck off, like I did.

Beauty radiates from the soul not the body carrying it. Your body is a mere vessel for this lifetime – what you choose to do with it or what you choose for it to look like, is completely and utterly your choice. At the end of the day it's your skin and your body – you are living in it, not the people who comment on it.

Yes, I have an ass that would make people jealous since there have been no ass injections involved.

No, I am not concerned about other people, because I like it and I am sure, one day, as Drake so eloquently put "someone will grab on that ass and firmly believe it".

Lesson of the Chapter

If your soul is ugly, your body makes no difference.

CHAPTER 14

White America

G irls and guys! It's 3:35AM and I am still writing. I might feel like throwing up soon, but I'll let you know if that happens.

How are you guys? I hope you are learning a ton of new facts. I am doing great.

Can you believe we are 28,000 words in? I think this was an amazing idea – I feel really good about writing some of this stuff down. It really is liberating. I had not done this before. I was so terrified of what people might say, but you know what? There are way too many people in the world and even in a person's life to try and please, without making yourself happy first.

Would you look at that! I dropped a lesson of the chapter before even beginning.

Okay let's get back to work. Don't worry, white people out there – I'm not going to spend all chapter hating on you, even though I'm am pretty sure you can take one for the team at this point.

I don't like Kohl's. The only reason I didn't say I hate Kohl's is because hate is a very strong emotion that Kohl's is not worthy of. To be fair, I don't like overly large stores, except for Target. Target is the shit.

I associate Kohl's with our overly stuffed vacation to Albania because that's where we bought most of our gifts and

I know, that also, is not their fault, but oh well. The store is huge. They don't know of any other colors in the rainbow except for shades of brown. You spend hours there for nothing. Everything is overpriced then "slashed" with their discounts. Ugh.

Out of all these reasons though there is one instance that stands out the most.

One day, my mom, my sister and I were in their shoe department. Another disappointment, as the never had size 11 in women for us giraffes out there. We had been chatting in Albanian, and believe me when I say we were very civil. Other Albanians will shout in public like a dog peeing in the park to mark his territory.

As we moved down the aisle, there was a woman and her daughter standing in the way, in not the nicest way. They could have flushed against the rack to let us pass or stayed on one side of the aisle, but no, they were spreading worse than a douche man-spreading on the subway. My mom very quietly excused herself to move past them.

Let the record show that my mom is very quiet and my sister inherited that whole appeasing thing from her – not that my sister had that characteristic anymore.

The woman didn't move – not even a centimeter. So, my mom slightly raised her voice and the daughter flipped out. Saying my mom didn't need to yell and how my mom was rude and uncultured, and then she said my mom should go back to Russia.

From Albania, With Love

Have you ever seen a lion attack their prey in the wild?

If you haven't, I'm sure you can imagine it or look it up on YouTube. You can also imagine that was me – only a few seconds after the girl finished her offensive and rude comments. I didn't physically assault her – the days of Berta were behind me, and my mother always says if you are going to kill someone, make sure they are worth the jail time.

I used my words. More like shouted them. Lots of profanities and a hell of a lot of threats using the mafia – white people are terrified of a mafia they don't know exists even more than they fear someone calling them a racist.

They basically ran out of the store and my mom was a little shocked. Not at the comments from the girl, but at my behavior. I told you, I'm a champ at internalizing, but something snapped. It was almost like when you see your mom cry – it cuts you off at the knees.

And, no it was not the first or last time something like that happen because ask any Albanian out there – they think Americans hate immigrants. We don't think Americans are ever going to accept us for who we are and some Albanians even believe Americans are bitter that we take their spots in schools, jobs, etc.

They aren't wrong.

If this is coming as a shock to you, believe me, not only are immigrants brilliant, but we can detect hate and tension in your faces when we discuss our successes. Unlike you, we don't make assumptions about you because you are different than us, or you practice another religion, or you don't look like us, or you don't have the same culture as us – we just automatically assume you dislike us because of those reasons and sometimes we go on the defensive.

Which brings me to a topic most people have mixed feelings about.

Freshman year roommate.

I don't know how they do it now since it's been almost three years since I graduated and seven years since freshman year – oh God, I feel old, but back in my day, we would receive our roommate's name along with a packet of info in the mail.

I got a first name and the first letter of a last name.

Great. Either she's weird or my university sucks and couldn't get her full last name. Is she some sort of serial killer?

Oh...the freshman year jitters – if only I had those sort of stressful thoughts now.

I put on my big girl pants and went on Facebook, as any normal human would, and creeped on my future roommate.

Let's call her Thea.

Thea was the whitest girl I had ever seen in my entire life.

I went to high school in a suburb of Massachusetts. I can count on my hands the amount of African American, Hispanic, and Asian students we had. Safe to say – I did not live around diversity. It was your typical white American town. My high school experience wasn't really something that stood out, but I mean who can really say they had the best time ever? It only lasts four years and then it's done – forever.

I never went to a high school party.

I never did any sort of drugs – including weed.

I never had a boyfriend.

I never really fit into a group.

I know what you're thinking. You're thinking I was prude or a nerd or an outcast, but I wasn't.

My high school never really seemed like the clique type. Sure, there were groups that hung out together; the athletes, the cheerleaders, the weed group, the science group, etc. I was always a combination of a lot of different things – I never liked sticking to a specific group, but I was friendly with most groups.

I took four AP classes, but I was not in the "we think we're so smart, we pretend other students don't exist" club.

I was the captain of my volleyball team, but I wasn't in the "jocks" club.

I liked artistic projects, but I was not in the "intimidating art student" club.

I loved reading and literature, but I was not in the "let's quote Shakespeare in everyday life" club.

I don't know if you guys believe in signs from the universe. For me, it sort of goes hand in hand with fate. Signs are like directional arrows from fate, telling you if you are in the right direction or not. Sometimes you don't even see them or maybe can't see them because you are hazy from what you are going through or maybe you just want to ignore them.

I know, I know. Some of you think I'm crazy for saying that, but I am a product of a highly superstitious family. I try not to latch on to it too much and it's not like I see a billboard for sky diving and go jump out of a plane.

My point goes back to the very beginning of this honest piece. I never saw the signs. The signs that I was never meant to fit in. From the moment, I split my head open, to being so desperate to fit in that I threw my lunch out, to high school and even through college, but the signs where always there. They now stick out in my brain like cautionary red flags in a mine field.

Sometimes, the signs are people.

My freshman year roommate was another sign.

I was accustomed to white people and how they felt about immigrants – obviously – but Thea and her family were like a J Crew catalog mixed with a Ralph Lauren ad type of white.

I furiously creeped through her Facebook page and the more I saw the more I started believing those horror stories Teen Vogue sometimes had in their magazines, about roommates.

Here's a picture of Thea and her perfect family in Florida. Here's a picture of Thea and her perfectly blond and fit friends. Here's a picture of Thea at the beach with model worthy looking guys. Here's a picture of Thea at the family business. Every single picture was decorated with a smile.

I know, people don't put pictures of depressing times online (well, actually – some people are super extra), but this girl seemed like the happiest, bubbliest, blondest, mean girl type material. AND, yes, that was me stereotyping out of fear, but then she messaged me.

Thea was very, very nice. Conversation flowed easily as we planned what to bring and what to share. Our messages were novel long. We would talk about our day, our plans, our high school experience and anything else you can think of.

I actually just reactivated my Facebook account to see those messages and when I tell you we wrote a LOT – if you transfer it to paper, each message was probably a page, single spaced.

Still, I was hesitant. Someone can sound very nice and a friendship can start out the best way and end horribly. Then there was the elephant in the room. Her parents.

I made up these situations in my head that they were mean, that they didn't like immigrants, that they would tell her to not speak to me or be rude to me. Overthinking at its best.

Dear God.

I am a very honest person, as you have seen and read, which means I am okay with saying I am wrong about something. I am not one of those people that can't ever admit when they are at fault. That being said – I am not wrong often, but when I am it's on a royal level.

To this day, as I sit here writing this, I have never met a nicer family. Thea's parents were and still are the best people. So welcoming, so warm, so open minded and accepting.

And Thea?

She was so interested in cultures other than her own. She loved the fact that I listened to Spanish music and wanted to learn the language too. I would teach her Albanian words – and yes, some were profanities. When my mom would make Albanian food, Thea was the first to try it, without making faces like some of my future roommates, by the way (girls I chose to live with). When it was my birthday, I came back from class to find a bouquet of flowers on my desk from Thea. When her mom sent her a care package, she would always include something for me. We would talk about any and everything. There was never a hint of jealousy, judgement, bitterness, clinginess, or hatefulness from Thea's voice and actions.

I won the roommate lottery. Sorry, everybody out there who had an awful experience.

Not to rub it in your face, but the family business Thea's parents had was ice cream. Homemade, fresh and delicious ice cream which Thea would bring back with her every time she would go home for the weekend.

I don't necessarily have the best feelings towards the university I went to (a story for later) but I will say, with 1000% assurance, I would do it all over again just to have Thea in my life.

From Albania, With Love

Why didn't Thea and I live together after freshman year?

That was the beauty of our friendship. We had our own life. We could be close friends while not being on top of each other. We had different classes, different friends, different organizations, and different interests, but that didn't take away from our friendship. Some people, like Naira, think a friendship is seeing or texting each other every moment. It's not – at least, not for me.

True friendship for me is simply someone you can be yourself with.....more than that, because sometimes it takes a while to figure out who yourself is – a true friend is someone you can tell anything to without feeling like they will judge you. You don't need to tell them everything, but you have the assurance that you can undoubtedly speak freely and just be you.

So, what sort of sign was Thea for me?

She was so free and happy even on the worse days. It was how I had always imagined myself – at least in my mind. The problem was I was protective, strong, and closed off – thick skinned and people saw that as angry, rough, mean, bitchy, dark. It was none of the things I wanted to be or thought I was. I always wanted to be happy, soft but assertive, protective but vulnerable, bright, thoughtful and just simply free to not give a shit what people thought I was.

Thea was that light for me. Just look up what the name Thea means.

I assumed she was so many things before I met her which turned out to be the complete opposite, but I ignored the red flags and just continued to step in mines.

Lesson of the Chapter

Give people a chance. They may just be what you don't know you need.

CHAPTER 15

$180,000 Fee

B iology was always my favorite scientific subject in school. English was my favorite of all – as you can imagine, but Biology fascinated me. I enjoyed learning about DNA, how the human body works, strange diseases – which reminds me of this project I had sophomore year. We had to research a rare disease and I found this one were a person suffers from extremely elastic skin and that was some graphic shit man.

Anyway, my love for science stopped at Biology. I extremely disliked Chemistry and I didn't mind Anatomy, but the teacher was a trip.

Physics was my mortal enemy. As if science wasn't bad enough, they had to go and add math. The worse part was that I took the class willingly.

At my high school, only two years of science was required, but I had a plan set since freshman year of high school. I would build up my résumé and classes to ensure I would get into the college I wanted. My sister and I went to the same college – both for business, so because she went four years ahead of me, she knew all the classes which would look good to the admissions office. I stopped playing the viola and took Accounting instead, and I took science all four years.

Oh, what's that? You didn't know I played an instrument?

Well I did. I played the viola for five years. I wanted to play the violin like all the other kids, but my arms were too long – the struggles of being tall – so, they gave me the viola. It's basically a slightly bigger version of the violin and it's deeper or lower in pitch.

It was all fun and games until that one time I had to tell my conductor that my G string broke. Can you say awkward?

My junior year of high school, I took the dreaded Physics course and I can say I hated every single second of it.

A bullet is moving at a speed of 365 m/s when it embeds into a lump of moist clay. The bullet penetrates for a distance of 0.0633 m. Determine the acceleration of the bullet while moving into the clay.

What the fuck is that?

It's safe to say that I stayed after school almost every day. Unlike my Anatomy teacher, my Physics teacher was actually funny. He was different, to put it in a nice way. He had a mixture of grey and black hair on the side and back of his head – the top was bald and he had muted brown eyes covered by large glasses. He sort of reminded me of a Walter White type of character. I'm pretty sure he had graduated MIT and went to Brown for graduate school, but decided to leave half way through. He made me wonder about life and how he ended up being a teacher in our town.

From Albania, With Love

I respect teachers – I don't know if I could ever do what they do, but let me remind you we were in a school district in which one teacher taught Italian and French.

One day after school he asked me about my plan for college and beyond. I don't know if he thought I wasn't going anywhere fast since I couldn't grasp even the simplest physics concept or he was just curious. Either way, he was another red flag.

You see, I had a plan set since freshman year of high school and probably even before that. I was going to business school to study Marketing. I was going to graduate and get a sick job in Boston, and then proceed to live like a character out of Sex and the City. Fabulous, young, and rich – I would feel accomplished. I was sure of it.

Notice how nowhere in there did you see the word happy?

I told him this plan sans the Sex and the City part and he laughed at me and said that is not going to happen. He didn't say it in a malicious manner, but I refused to believe him. I was convinced I would make it happen. He didn't doubt I would, but he asked me:

"What if you change your mind? What if you realize that it's not for you?"

I firmly shook my head. I knew it was for me. I would never change my mind. It was the life I wanted!

Remember immigrant child syndrome? Here is exactly how it works.

I needed to be perfect for my parents. I needed to fit in for my own good.

I only applied to one university – I didn't even visit other ones, didn't even think about what sort of job I wanted after I was done with school. I applied early decision, which meant if I got in, I promised to go. It was a decision I did not think about – it was the plan, the plan that would make my parents proud and maybe they would finally feel like the sacrifice they made was all for something.

Once I got to college, I declared my major almost immediately. The same major as my sister with a few differences.

International Business (IB) & Marketing with a minor in French.

The French part was required. If you majored in IB, you had to minor in a language. It was their way of preparing you – or so to speak – for the real world.

It was actually a tactic for them to ensure people got jobs after graduating. A language is impressive. Impressive meant you get a job. You getting the job meant higher post grad results for the University. Higher results meant more students attending. More students attending meant more money.

Money is always the objective.

Lucky for me, spring semester freshman year, I ended up having a horrid French TA as my professor. To say I was annoyed is an understatement. I woke up at 6AM to make sure I got the professor I wanted and instead I ended up with a TA who was too busy flirting with the only guy in the class – not cute, by the way – and she also spend about 20 minutes, each class, reading her poems out loud to us to practice her English.

You would think I was happy about the distraction, but I didn't necessarily appreciate spending $4,000 for a class so my TA can read poems about death and sex.

Yep... that was her topic – all the fucking time.

The head of the department refused to do anything because the TA needed the hours of experience to complete her program, as if that was my fucking problem, so I took matters into my own hands.

No, I didn't do something mean or spiteful. Relax.

I did some research and realized that I didn't have to take French for my major, IF I could take a test and prove that I spoke another language fluently. I told you – English being my second language has nothing but benefits.

The university I went to prides themselves in a well-rounded education so freshman year was mostly the same for all students, including English courses which I enjoyed very much. When I placed out of French, I decided to make my major something English related.

I needed a break from all the business. My courses consisted of Finance, Marketing, Accounting, Management, Micro & Macro Economics. I was drowning while internalizing.

I made my minor Professional and Creative Writing.

Spring semester, sophomore year I took a class called Writing For Publication 451. The number at the end meant the class was a high level/ more difficult. It was intimidating at first as everybody was either a junior or a graduating senior, but I was glad to get a break from all my business classes.

The professor was an older woman, who I had not heard the best about. Rumored to be an amazing professor, but tough as shit. The type of tough that reads your work and makes you edit out loud, in front of the class.

Pause.

I loved English, but I didn't have the best experience with teachers in high school post sophomore year. I had the best teacher my sophomore year – it was in his class that I discovered how much I love writing fiction, but after that it was downhill.

First there was junior year with a teacher who looked like he should have been the gym teacher or the football coach. He made us take spelling quizzes each week like we were in elementary school. After him, I briefly had a teacher almost all the "literature loving" girls thought was the most attractive man they had ever seen.

Nope. Not even close.

Due to my schedule, I switched to the last teacher of my high school career. She was the tough teacher. You know the one who would deduct a whole point for a grammatical error or would only give out Bs as not to lose her status as the tough teacher. Now, I know that was not her intention and I

From Albania, With Love

understand I was not the best writer back then, but I literally
tried everything. No matter how differently I analyzed
Dante's Inferno, apparently, it was never better than a B.

I guess that should have been my hint that I was
meant for fictional writing, in which I could write however I
pleased, and not for the perfectly structured analytical writing
world.

Play.

Our first assignment of the Writing for Publication
class was to write a memory. Pick a memory from the past
and write about it, in any way you want. The best thing she
said on the first day of class?

*"I don't care about grammar. You write how you
feel. If one word needs to be your sentence to make a point
then so be it."*

Best thing to tell a writer. Ever.

I mean, she still expected it to make sense – this isn't
abstract art, but even with the freedoms she gave us, I was
having a hard time getting the piece to say what I wanted it to
say. It was personal – I wrote about the day we left Albania. I
always seemed to go back to that, whether I realized or not.
Most times I didn't.

The two times a writer, like myself, feels like they
are sitting on needles is when someone reads their work out
loud, and when you are sitting in the room as someone is
silently reading your work while their facial expression
changes numerous times. That's what my professor did, when

I went to see her during office hours – she sat in silence and read.

I stared.

When she finished, she set the pages down on her very crowded desk and asked me a question I was not expecting.

"What are you doing when you graduate?"

"W – what do you mean?" I stuttered because I still had two years to figure that shit out. I didn't need people asking that question prematurely.

"You know – in a few months when you graduate?"

"I'm only a sophomore…"

My professor was a petite woman with a hoarse voice, - sort of like she smoked a pack a day. She reminded me of my grandma, not because my grandma smoked, but because when she got excited she perked up in her seat like my professor did. She went on to talk extremely fast and tell me that I *NEED* to tell my story. I *NEED* to use my voice. She was convinced I needed to tell my story of immigration and use my different outlook to communicate with people. She told me that she thought I was a senior because of the way I carried myself and my writing style.

It was the greatest compliment anybody gave me on my writing, but at that moment, I thought she *NEEDED* some pills.

Why?

1st. Nobody cares to read about immigration.

2nd. Why would people care about my story? There are millions of immigrants.

3rd. My parents would have a heart attack if I suddenly became an English major.

4th. Writing will not make me successful. Starving artist much?

5th. People would be mad if I wrote about them.

6th. People would not like it or care.

And on, and on, and on.

I could not make my parents proud if I didn't get a business diploma and get that secure job. Their sacrifice would be worth nothing and all the hard work I had put into getting my IB degree would go out the window for some flaky career.

Still, it imprinted an idea in my mind and I thought about it for a few days. I even got the paper work to switch majors and like any other insecure college kid who was more concerned with what people thought than my own life, I asked my "friends" what they thought. I should probably add here that I did not have a single friend in the Bachelor of Arts program.

Money. That was all their answer accumulated too and the fact that I would find no job after graduation. Their voices were laced with jokes about me as a future librarian and my mind was clouded with a simple fact I told you earlier.

Albanians aren't quitters. The IB program at the university I graduated is one of the toughest in the country.

We began with 250 students enrolled and only 60 graduated with the degree. I was not about to become one of the ones who could not handle it and I simply could not disappoint my parents.

As much as I disliked business, as much as I liked English, as much as I hated math, as much as I felt no excitement about working in an office, and as much as I sometimes struggled in my courses – I could not let them down and make their sacrifice be worth nothing.

Lesson of the Chapter

If you let it, guilt can manifest to regret.

CHAPTER 16

Number 2 Won't Do

I never liked Columbus Day – even if it did grant me a day off or a long weekend. I mean, who really likes Columbus Day or what it "celebrates"? I have always felt so awkward around it and frankly I never understood why it deserves a national day…one of the many things which still baffle me about the US.

And then, there is the whole Columbus Day sale thing. If you celebrate what the day is about – then it basically means I can walk into your store, take what I want and walk out.

There's an idea.

Fall semester, junior year was slow on campus. Well, as far as the IB program was concerned anyways. You see, not only was the IB program extremely tough, but it was also strictly structured.

Freshman and sophomore year, we took our core classes while also completing our minor. Then fall semester, junior year, everybody went abroad as required to complete the program and get a degree. Most people went in a country which spoke the language they were taking. The university liked to tell you the limits were endless, but trying to find classes – say in Scotland – was impossible. Additionally, if you dared ask to go somewhere else, you basically had to petition, because you know – it wasn't our money or anything.

Usually, Spanish minors went to Seville, Spain or Grenada, Spain; French minors went to Paris, France or Aix – En – Provence, France; Chinese minors went to Shanghai, China or Beijing, China.

Just like in high school, there were more Spanish minors than anything else.

The Spanish minors – about 40 – all went to Spain that fall. They all lived either in the same apartment building with a house mother or just a few blocks away from each other. They went to work together, lived together, attended school together and partied together. Sounds like fun, right?

Nope.

At least not for me. I was at the "I need space from everybody" stage at that point in my college career and life. When I went abroad – I wanted it to be just me and new people. I was fed up with the ones around me, but there was a slight hint of need. Like it would have been fun for about one weekend.

When they returned from abroad, we all dove head into spring semester. It was the most brutal semester for IB majors. In groups of four, we all competed against each other as well as other universities in a virtual business game. That year, the game was in the sneaker industry. Each of us formulated a company and then we made all the decisions. How much we paid our employees, legal problems, celebrity endorsement, production issues, pricing, marketing, finance, safety – literally like running a real-life Nike and dealing with every single department.

Each week we would make decisions and on Sunday the results would come out based on how the simulated market was doing, and based on how mean our professors wanted to be. They could fluctuate prices or tell us there was a fire in our production factory or suddenly, a celebrity endorsement went south because the celebrity did drugs.

Real life shit and brutal for the students that just got back from partying in France, China, and Spain.

As I mentioned before the IB program was small so everybody knew everybody. When it came to formulating groups – everybody wanted the best because everybody wanted to win, even if there was no real prize involved. I adored my group. Three of us had been a group freshman year and by the time junior year rolled around, we found a fourth member.

It was obviously me and let's call the other three Lucy, Nicholas, and Scott.

Lucy and I went to high school together and even played volleyball one year. We handled the marketing and management aspect – we both loved visuals and presentation.

Nicholas was the type of man you want to bring home to mom, but at the same time would get into a fight for you if he needed to. Added plus, he was funny and incredibly smart.

I know what you're thinking…*Ouuu, you liked him.*

Sure, I won't lie – when I first met him and got to know him, I thought he was great, and he was cute, but the moment he mentioned his girlfriend – immediate friendship. I don't do that – ever, and I also don't pine over someone. Once I establish a guy is simply a great friend – I care about him, I want him to be happy. Truly.

Last, but not least, Scott. Scott was the nicest guy I met my whole college career. He kept to himself and he could work wonders with a computer or a spreadsheet, but every once in a while, he would crack jokes and it was honestly the best remedy for working on a group project until midnight.

Why am I mentioning them?

I think you realize by now that I don't necessarily have the best attitude or feeling towards the university I attended. I mean, my time there was alright and I am sure this is coming as a huge surprise to anybody who knew me when I was there. I appeared to love it when I attended.

Internalizing champ, remember?

AND, yes – trust me, I know it was my choice to go there, but certain factors have made me deeply regret actions I took in the past (*I will explain – I promise*). As I look back on it now, I like to, and I think it's important to remember the good times. I learned the hard way that you can't take back time, so I try and remember the good instead of the bad.

Those people – Nicholas, Scott, and Lucy – and that semester we spent every waking moment together was actually fun. I felt like I belonged somewhere, but not in a wanting to fit in type of way. Just natural happiness in the middle of extremely difficult work. I actually felt accomplished and I think it helped that we finished in first place every week.

We fucking dominated.

So, why didn't I study abroad in the fall of junior year?

My minor did not allow for me to take the classes I needed to, in order to complete it in time. That's the lie I told everybody – including my parents.

The truth?

I failed Statistics.

I told you I would be honest.

My fall semester, sophomore year was extremely packed. I was taking five courses; Statistics, Consumer Behavior, History of Modern Europe, Math 106, Advertising Management. I was part of three major campus organizations. I also had a job on campus, Monday through Friday, from 11:30 until 2:30.

How do I remember all this? I still have the excel of my schedule on my laptop.

I'm extra like that.

The same fall, my dad had a physical exam. Routine – nothing to worry about until they found a spot on his leg. When I say my dad's doctor is a major idiot and should probably get her medical license revoked, I'm not kidding. Instead of testing for other possibilities, like a normal human being, she tells my parents, who still don't really understand English well, that my dad might have cancer.

145

And they say jealous females jump to conclusions. She fucking leaped.

I drove home about six times in a span of a month and a half. I spoke to every single doctor – as my mom of course, because they only speak to the spouse. I scheduled appointments, I translated, I interpreted and as a result my grades plummeted. It just so happened that doctors would call when I was in statistics class, so I would step out and talk to them for about five to ten minutes and then I would call my mom and console her, comfort her, reassure her for 15 to 20 minutes. I would guarantee that my dad did not have cancer and that he was not dying even though I didn't really know at that point.

Maybe others are better at juggling that much at once, but I made a decision. Clearly statistics was not my strongest subject to begin with, so I let it fall to the side and made sure I was all set in my other courses as well as taking care of my parents – I owed them.

When his final results were ready, my mom called me hysterical saying that the radiology office was saying their system was down and they could not get the scans to the doctor until after the holiday. My mom is not a patient woman, and her mind goes into over drive when things are elongated. She starts to think they are doing it on purpose because it's bad news. I couldn't deal.

I was already failing and now they wanted to give me some 1990 excuse?

Fuck no.

From Albania, With Love

I left work early that day – the Friday of Columbus Day weekend – after I bitched out the radiology department and they told me I could come and take the films and deliver them to the doctor myself. That's what I did.

I hopped in my car and drove 45 miles to get the fucking floppy disk and then delivered it to the doctor. It turned out to be built calcium, by the way – not cancer.

By the time I got around to looking at what I needed to pass my statistics class, it was useless. I needed to get something ridiculous – like 140% on my final. Impossible.

I took a large, bold F on my final grade and my GPA plummeted extremely low.

That's always how it works, isn't it? Four great grades raise you GPA by .04, but one bad grade drops it by a whole fucking point, and you spend the rest of your college career attempting to fix a pricey mistake that wasn't even entirely your fault.

Kind of ironic if you think about it.

I went to that expensive school to make them proud and I was failing so I could take care of them. It was an expensive way to make them happy, but the immigrant child syndrome is an unrelenting bitch.

Lesson of the Chapter

Learn from the darkness of the past, but hold only the
bright spots in your heart.

CHAPTER 17

That Underground Hip Hop Club

T oday, we start with fun facts.
Side Bar.
It's actually Wednesday. I know I said I would give myself until Monday at midnight to finish this, but did you actually think writing that many words, pages, and stories is that simple? If you did – you have a lot to learn (in future chapters) about how writing a story works.

Back to facts.

Fact # 1 – Once I have made up my mind, it's close to impossible to change it.

Fact # 2 – I am not like most people.

I can almost hear all the guys reading this, groaning in the background – like they haven't heard a girl say that before? More than likely they have heard it from an ex-girlfriend who turned out to be completely psycho. The "I made a scrapbook of what our kid would look like" type of psycho. Guys usually can't win – they don't think they understand women and they think whatever they do won't help. Here's a hint, fellas. Why don't you try and understand us as human beings rather than women?

That's the problem – isn't it?

Every time you get into a fight with your girlfriend and you talk about it with your friends – the first thing that comes out of your mouth is "Women, right?"

Wrong.

Believe it or not, women are human and no two humans are the same, but I don't blame you because men are simple, so you think it's a gender thing – like somehow having a vagina makes us more prone to being emotional, sensitive, clingy, and willing to spring into a fight over nothing. You also probably have categories for us – boxes that we can fit into that ultimately mean we are something else.

A girl who sleeps around has daddy issues.

A girl who doesn't sleep around is prude.

A girl who is funny is probably ugly.

A girl who is ugly has a great personality.

A girl who reads a lot is a nerd and not exciting.

A girl who doesn't read is stupid.

A girl who has a lot of friends is insecure.

A girl who doesn't have any friends is weird.

A girl who demands what she wants is bossy.

A girl who doesn't know what she wants is annoying.

A girl who doesn't rely on you is not feminine.

A girl who relies on you is too clingy.

I mean this is fucking exhausting – it's no wonder you always seem to be wrong about women. If you actually took the time to just get to know someone, instead of implying that they will be a certain way because they fit into this category of woman or that category of woman, then you would save yourself so much time and so many headaches.

Don't look at me like that. You know it's true.

AND, yes – we also have categories for you men out there: mamma's boy, gym freak, bad boy, preppy with a hint of "my dad's a lawyer", old fashioned, nerdy, social media obsessed, and on and on and on.

The difference between how men think of women and how women think of men is that while – at first appearance – you might seem to fit one of those categories, us women, still get to know you as a human being. Whether you deserve it or not, because you see, yes, we may have daddy issues or not have the best examples of men in our past, but somehow, we can still give men a chance in hopes that they will prove us wrong.

I know the large problem here is society and no, I will not go into a large rant here, but just think of this:

When something bad happens to a woman and people tell a man – "well, imagine if that was your mom or sister" – to get him to feel bad.

Who in the fuck cares if he has a mom or sister?

Right is right and wrong is wrong. Respect women because they deserve it like any other human being, and especially like women respect men without giving it a second thought, because it's the fucking normal thing to do until people prove you wrong.

Now, I am not sitting here ranting about male female relations and making men seem terrible, because I know most of them aren't. I have had a few good ones in my life, but consider this a sort of prelude to the next chapter and a way to get to know me a bit more.

Let me explain.

Remember the immigrant child syndrome? Of course, you do.

There are two ways a daughter of an immigrant can go – specifically an Albanian immigrant. I say daughter because, I am obviously a woman.

Here's the story.

In the first chapter of this collection of honest stories, I talked about Albanian history – past tense. I don't know how much you know about Albania now, but those same things I told you about peoples' stereotypes that we are all criminals, or aggressive, or Russian, or corrupt, or a third world country…. they all stand, because people don't know.

Current events Albania doesn't really matter in this story. Albania is a beautiful country with a lot to offer the world. It is still a corrupt country as politics always are, but they are more open with it. Were America would have Olivia Pope to cover their scandals, Albania would have politicians just saying – "Hey, man, yeah I did it? What are you gonna do?"

Obviously, they are a bit more refined in the way they say it, but you get the idea.

Now, I'll remind you that Albania was closed off from the world for 44 years, so ideals of freedom – gender, sexuality, and speech – were not so diverse or free – if you will.

Why am I reminding you of this?

You know when you read a book or watch a movie and you see this character who is strange or off putting or even a villain? I always wonder why they are like that – what could have happened that made him/her that way. You see, people always think the main character is normal, but what really constitutes normal? Is it a behavior or a background or the way they look?

Example: With or without knowing it, I was a disappointment since the day I was born. The people I was supposed to trust most – my family – wanted me to be something else from the moment I drew my first breath.

Other girls in Albania may not have been born into that, but here is what I know they were raised with:

Women being unable to drive due to society's judgement. Women being unable to express their sexuality without being called whores. Women being unable to have a life and be single without being shamed. A woman's only duty being a wife and a mother. Not a single example of a woman in any sort of powerful caliber such as politics, arts, science, etc.

Don't believe me?

When we came to the states, my dad thought he was living in an alternative universe when he saw a man changing a baby's diaper.

When we went on our vacation to Albania, my dad blamed the turbulence on the plane on the pilot, because women shouldn't have that job.

When I was younger, my dad would not make his bed in the morning because that was a woman's job.

I think you get my point.

So, now, imagine being raised like that and then coming to the United States. I know what you're going to say, but please spare me. Yes, the US has a lot of fixing to do in the women equality department, however, here there is freedom, here there are examples, here there are men who don't think a woman is a possession, and here is the option to do whatever you please. AND, yes, people might judge you, but at least you have the options.

There are two ways this can go for daughters of Albanian immigrants.

1. Over The Top Independence - Once you are old enough to realize you have options and freedoms, you lash out. You take advantage of those options and do everything you could not imagine doing in Albania. You have numerous boyfriends, you swear at your parents, you hang out with the wrong crowds, you wear things your parents don't approve of, you party, you don't go to school, etc.

2. You Become Your Parents – Some people can't shake how they were raised. When you come to the States, you realize what your parents go through and the freedoms this country grants you so you figure you will do everything in your power to be perfect for your parents – reach heights they never could in Albania. You get straight As, you never have a boyfriend, you never drink or do drugs, you hang out with proper kids, you go to an amazing college, you get a

properly boring husband and have kids. Long story short –
you become an upgraded version of your parents.

Did you notice how, no matter which of the two
paths chosen, it was not a decision made for an individual?
You are either choosing to become your parents or resent
your parents. It's a difficult shadow to come out of and I
know you're wondering which of the two I chose.... well,
actually, maybe you think it's number one since I am writing
this piece, but it was sort of both.

I did everything for my parents. I had too. They
brought me to the magnificent United States of America and
no, I'm not being sarcastic. From eight years old, when I got
here, until right about 21 years old, when I studied abroad, I
had chosen path number two.

I was perfect, or at least I tried to be.

I learned how to read financial reports and balance
checkbooks when other kids were experiencing their first kiss
in middle school. I went to every single doctor's appointment
my parents had when other kids were going to after school
activities. I opened all their credit cards and accounts while
other kids were going to parties. I filled out paper work for
my family to visit us in the US when other kids were going to
the beach over the summer. I handled my mom's insurance
paper work, while I also tried to be volleyball captain and get
through high school. I completed all the refinancing
paperwork for the house when my friends were going on
spring break. I called every bill, if there was ever a
discrepancy, even while attempting to complete my college

degree. I took out $180,000 in loans, after they paid all they could for my sister's college, as to not put that sort of pressure on them.

I did it all and it still never felt like enough. I never felt like enough.

The summer before my senior year of college, I finally studied abroad. Where I went was up to me since I had placed out of French and no longer took a language, but I still wanted to go to France. I had always wanted to go to Paris, but the only program available that summer was in Aix – En – Provence. It was a seven-week program and I was to stay with a family.

Even though it wasn't Paris, I was super excited to go.

Remember I told you I love to travel? Well, this trip almost caused me to have a heart attack. My flights were fine; I flew from Boston to Dublin, then from Dublin to Marseille. The problem was the layover and Aer Lingus's poor scheduling. I only had 40 minutes to get through security, run through an international airport and board my flight to Marseille.

Great.

By the time I got to security, I only had 25 minutes to get to my gate and there were at least 30 people in front of me. I didn't know what I was going to do if I missed my flight. It wasn't just the money aspect, but it was also the whole group (abroad program) would leave at a certain time if I didn't get there.

I can only imagine what I looked like – probably like I had seen a ghost mixed with on the brink of a panic attack, topped off with the complexion of someone who was about the throw up. The best part of Dublin and the only part I saw, were the people. One of the TSA officers approached me and I thought he was going to yell about something – it was the last thing I needed.

"Are you okay?"

That's what he actually said in an amazing Irish accent and everything. I know, I know. I am one of those people that is a sucker for accents, but I'm particular – nothing American, and while I love London, I think Irish and, even better, Scottish accents are just the best.

No, it doesn't mean I am going to start stripping my clothes off for you, but it helps. I can understand people who don't get it though – people tell me I have an accent, and I can never hear it.

Anyway, it wasn't just the accent. He took me out of the line and let me pass through security – I skipped everybody else and made my flight just in time.

So, thanks, officer cutie.

Arriving to Marseille was strange – sort of like when I went to China, but this time it was closer to home – both in distance and familiarity. I was composed and calm, as always, but inside I was terrified. I was the only one there from my whole university – not just the IB program. I knew nobody. I was going to live with a family I knew nothing about except the fact that it was a mom and her young daughter. AND, there would be two other girls living in the house with me.

You know how I said up until I was 21 years old, I fit into path number 2?

Well, Aix – En – Provence changed my prospective.

No, I didn't all of a sudden become a sex fiend – clubbing and drinking like a wild woman because I was abroad. It was a different prospective – just listen.

I was exhausted when we finally arrived to the house. The flight. The running through Dublin. The walking through the cobble stone streets. My heavy ass luggage. You get it, but apparently, my new housemate did not. Let's call her Blair.

Blair had been there for the Spring semester already, but she was staying a few more weeks to complete her internship. She was like a living Barbie doll. Blonde, blue eyes, a warm smile, and cheery – very cheery, and thankfully very nice. Blair had a French boyfriend. Of course.

The moment I put my bags down, Blair wanted to know what I was doing. Normally I would have been annoyed – I like my space – but I didn't mind. I wanted to go exploring since our other roommate was getting there later on in the day.

The weather was perfection and the city seriously reminded me of a scene out of Beauty and the Beast. There was a fresh market in the town center every morning. Blair and I walked around the open tented market surrounded by small shops and bakeries.

From Albania, With Love

Blair separated from me for a minute to pick out some cherries and I looked around. It was at that moment, I realized how much I missed Albania. The markets my grandma and I would go to and the free feeling you have as a child that you don't even realize until you aren't free. Everything around me was so simple, so small – just right there in the moment. No rush to become something, someone or make a shit ton of money. I imagined living like that. Living for the moment, being surrounded by things I loved without being afraid of it – nobody there knew me. I could be whoever I wanted. I was free of this person everybody had made up their mind I was, just because I was tough, closed off, dark, and complex.

I could breathe – I felt so free and I remembered that's what happy felt like.

Our last housemate and my official roommate had been doing a Euro trip with her boyfriend and her best friend. Her last stop was Aix – En – Provence for a five-week architecture program. Let's call her Serena.

That first night, our house mom made us a quiche. I still have the recipe and make it from time to time – it was to die for. After drinking two bottles of wine between the six of us, even though I wasn't tired, I wanted to go to bed. It was 11PM and I had been up for more than 20 hours at that point, but Blair did not care.

"Your first night here!? We are going out!"

That's what she screamed excitedly at both me and Serena, so out we went. By the way, this was unlike me. I don't like clubs, I don't like darkness, I don't like strangers dancing up on me. I don't like tight outfits. I don't like paying $20 for a drink.

Freshman year was mostly drinking in your dorm room and trying not to get caught going to a senior party, which I never tried too hard with. I don't like seeming desperate, especially for an overcrowded party with sticky floors.

Sophomore year was a bit freer for partying since we had a suite, but I was too busy failing statistics to party.

Junior year was taken up by the extremely difficult IB program even though, I did go out once or twice.

Long story short – I didn't go to very many parties my first three years of college, and once again it goes back to immigrant child syndrome. Here I am going to a party and getting wasted when my parents sacrificed everything for me to get an education…. *ohh, the guilt.*

First, we went to an overcrowded bar – all of us. Blair, Blair's French boyfriend, Serena, Serena's boyfriend, Serena's best friend and me. We drank a tower of beers and then we went bar hopping until we ended up at this underground hip hop club. The entrance was scarier than being underground – it was guarded by some biker guys in leather jackets, but Blair knew them, so they let us go in without paying the cover. Don't let the Barbie persona fool you – Blair could get along with anybody.

The inside of the club was strangely set up. It looked like a cave – which, are not my favorite. It was dark with shades of blue and green lights everywhere and the left back corner was the make shift dance floor. The bar was modern – all glass, sort of like a weird version of an ice bar.

You would think this place would be my worst nightmare; dark surroundings, loud music, people dancing on each other, expensive drinks, and small spaces. I was fine. I was more than fine – I wasn't thinking about anything else as we made our way into the dance floor.

Out of left field – well more like the right side of the dance floor – a guy came over and started dancing with me.

Let me tell you, in France people don't grind like they do in America.

You know – when the guy just stands there and the girl's ass does most of the work – sometimes his hands just hang limply by his side and sometimes he holds the girl's hips. In France or maybe it was just this guy, they like front contact – a dancing position in which you can feel everything, especially when someone becomes excited to be against you.

Sorry mom.

It's safe to say this guy knew how to dance, so what do you think happened next?

He kissed me.

Let it go on record that French men know how to kiss as well. Very well. So, you are probably thinking, *yeah? So what? Plenty of people go dancing abroad or even stateside and make out with a stranger.*

Well, let it also go on the record that it was my first kiss.

Gasp! But, you were 21 years old?!

Yeah, I know how to do that math too. AND, yes there are people out there that haven't had their first kiss yet – we are like a rare breed of unicorns. It wasn't that I was waiting for the perfect guy or some sort of romantic way to have my first kiss – I just hadn't gotten around to it. I told you I didn't party much, and I never saw the point in making out with random dudes when I did go to these parties.

Was I sad about it? Nope.

Did I feel left out? Nope.

Most people have their first kiss in middle school or high school – well, now a day people are wild, but you get my point. During those times and even college, I was either taking care of my parents, lessening everybody else's problems, making sure my grades were tip top, or something else. My mind just wasn't on that.

The guilt. It can kill everything sometimes.

I fell squarely into the trying to be my parents path until that night in Aix – En – Provence.

It wasn't the fact that I had been kissed for the first time – I wasn't that shocked. It was the freedom. After the club, I left with my new friends/roommates and we walked around the city, just talking and letting the summer air into our lungs. Before we went home, we stopped at a local bakery (open 24/7) and got some chocolate croissants. When we got home, we remembered we had left our keys inside the house.

Serena's best friend – a sweet boy from Texas – scaled the building to get into the kitchen window. Between the laughing and munching on the warm croissants – I am pretty sure we stopped some of our neighbors mid sex, but it's okay, they could afford a night off.

Seriously, my next-door neighbors had sex all the time. Morning, night and even mid-day. I'd come home after class and hear the woman's moans bounce from the other apartment walls and yet, they had the fucking nerve to tell my Serena and I to stop talking one night at 11PM.

That first night was easily the best night of my life. I think everybody needs to have a night like that – not because we drank, or danced, or kissed, but because we didn't think. I didn't think about anything else, anybody else, but what I wanted. It was a freedom I had not known before. With every single decision I had ever made, I always thought how others would feel or react – I never thought how I would react or feel.

The rest of the trip was like that too. Freedom.

It helped that I was the only one from my university there and my housemates did not cling. We all did our own thing. I explored whatever I wanted. Went where I wanted. Ate what I wanted. All without someone else's input. All my choices, by me and for me.

Oh, and if you are wondering about the guy I had my first kiss with – no, I never saw him again. I know what you were expecting.

One day, I am shopping in the open tent market and we both grab the same orange and look up to see each other, but don't recognize each other. He asks me out and we have a grand dinner date. Things go along smoothly – a summer romance montage rolls on screen complete with bike rides through some random ass field, eating croissants at a beautiful park, and somehow making picnics look comfortable, visiting local galleries, museums, and historical spots, eating ice cream while kissing. It's all grand until he finds out I was that girl at the club and he is hurt I left him after he kissed me, but when I tell him he was my first kiss – he is touched and gives some cheesy speech about how these past few weeks have been the best ones of his life.

Seriously guys?

That's the cheesiest shit I have ever written and no, none of it happen. I never even got his name. I told you this is real life. No happy endings, yet.

Lesson of the Chapter

It's okay to put yourself first and not feel a shred of guilt about it.

From Albania, With Love

CHAPTER 18

First Love, First Jackass

I have always believed I have a sixth sense. Not in the weird I can see dead people type of way, but a heightened sense of first impressions. I get a vibe from someone – I know instantly if I am going to end up liking them or wanting nothing to do with them. It has never failed me, even though I have ignored it a few times.

And, no, I don't discount someone because I get a bad vibe from them. I give them a chance and see where it goes. Usually, it goes exactly where I was expecting.

You remember I told you fate gives us red flags, that we usually ignore? Well, buckle up. This story is full of land mines.

I didn't get a good vibe from Roman.

No, that is not his real name. Yes, I did pick a name I am not a fan off. Just look up to the chapter title for reference as to how this will end.

I didn't play volleyball in college. Our school became Division 1 the year I started and the combination of the rough IB program and the bitchiness from the other girls who played was enough for me to just stick to recreational volleyball.

That's where I first saw him – at a recreational volleyball game. He was playing for the same team and he had come there with a girl who would end up being a really

close friend of mine. Let's call her Sophie. I had known
Sophie since freshman year, but we had different groups of
friends, so we had never really hung out.

At first glance, Roman was everything a girl would
want. He had sparkling brown eyes, thick dark hair, an
infectious smile, long and dark eyelashes that sort of made me
jealous. He was great at sports. He was a top-grade student.
He was involved in lots of campus activities. He was a
resident advisor which meant he didn't go out every weekend,
get plastered and have sex with a multitude of different girls.
And, to top it all off, he had a great sense of style.

Still, I didn't get the vibe I was supposed to.

The way he carried himself was confident, but on the
brink of cocky. Without knowing all the details, I gave you
above, you would think he was a douche. Good looking,
quick on his feet and in high demand by every girl in his
building.

Red flag #1.

I don't like cocky guys. I hate guys who boost – as I
said, fine line between confident and cocky. I despised guys
who walked around campus like they were God's gift to earth
just because they were good looking or most girls would fall
at their feet. I would not be those girls.

Remember, last chapter, I told you I am not like
most people?

Well here you go.

I am a very private person – believe it or not –
especially when it concerns my private life and relationships.

From Albania, With Love

Whatever happens between me and my boyfriend, or any relationship, is nobody's business, but ours. You will never catch me writing some bullshit on Instagram like:

"Out of all the 7 billion people in the world, I am so happy I met you. You are my sunshine. You complete me and make my days worth living. I love you so much baby. I can't wait for our journey together. Happy Birthday!"

What. The. Actual. Fuck.

Before you tell me I'm bitter or a hater – please save your breath. I do believe in self-expression and living your life, but if you want your boyfriend or girlfriend to know he is your world then show him/her or tell him/her. Privately. Those photos and word are nothing but vanity.

Look at me! I'm in a relationship!

Yay! How great for you. Why don't you go and have the relationship instead of looking for affirmation from a bunch of strangers online? Do you think Jay Gatsby walked down the streets of New York and held a picture of him and Daisy and shouted at people to like it, while telling them how great she was?

No.

He fucking bought a house across from her and showed how much he loved her. Granted Daisy was a bitch in the end – you get my point.

Don't get me wrong – of course I would wish my boyfriend happy birthday with a picture of us, but the paragraphs aren't necessary. I like to show my love instead of show it off.

Remember this little rant. It will be helpful later.

It was fall semester my senior year when I first saw Roman.

That same semester I was directing a cultural show on campus – I did it all, folks. Sophie and Roman were part of the show, so after practice I would walk back to the dorms with them. My town house was just a few minutes away from their building. Both of them were resident advisors in the same building. It became habit and I still had feelings of freedom from being abroad – I needed distance from my town housemates. I had lived with some of them for three years and it wasn't that they were bad – I just enjoyed Sophie and Roman's company more.

Spring semester, things escalated.

I rarely went to my town house that semester. When Roman was on duty, I would sit at the desk and do homework with him. When Roman wasn't on duty, we would be in his room and do homework. I saw his gentleness, his willingness to put others before himself, his kindness with the people he was responsible for, and the way he had become a great example to many students.

This is when you roll the mid movie montage.

We walked to class together. We went on shopping runs together. We went to the library together. I would text him so we could meet for lunch in between classes. We would talk about our future dreams late into the night even when I had 8AM classes. Long hugs every time we saw each other and even longer walks when we had something on our mind.

I know, stage five clinger. *Completely* unlike me.

Red flag #2.

It was different and new. I just felt happy when I was with him, without even thinking about it. I would get those annoying butterflies in my stomach every time I saw him. I didn't care that my friend, Marina didn't like that I was spending so much time with him. We never said anything, but I figured he must feel something because I would catch him looking at me when he didn't think I noticed.

Hollywood ruins everything.

It was more than that though. We understood each other as we both had immigrant parents. Roman wanted to go into communications – more specifically he wanted to join the likes of Jimmy Fallon one day and I truly believed he could do it. He had the personality, the story, the drive, but he also had the fear.

Remember? If you want to give your immigrant parents a heart attack then you tell them you want to go into the arts, but still I encouraged him, even though I had no idea what I wanted to do myself. I thought it was important for him to follow his heart. I just wanted to see him happy.

Famous last words.

People started talking, of course. Small campus, big mouths. I don't blame them though, I would have thought the same thing. We were always together and when I had my 8AM class I would sleep over his room. Just sleep. Though, most people thought we did more than sleep, and the fact that he had a single room, and I would walk out of his building in the morning wearing his sweater did not help ease the rumors. I didn't care.

Honestly, I love when people jump to conclusions because nobody but I know what actually happened.

One day, I was packing up my things to head to my Writing Fiction class and Roman begged me not to go.

"Just stay with me, please."

My heart skipped. What guy who doesn't like you would say shit like that. Friends let you go to class – people who are interested in you say shit like that so they can spend more time with you.

Red flag #3.

I skipped class to stay with him. A class I was paying $4,000 for, and it wasn't just the money, it was the act. I very rarely skipped class and I never skipped just because I didn't feel like going. *AND*, I liked that class. I'm sure you can imagine why.

Roman was happy so I was happy…until he pulled out his phone and Tweeted about the fact that he convinced me to skip class.

Red flag #4.

He was a social media whore, and my gut knew it, but my heart told me he is tweeting because he is telling the world that we are spending time together. My social media rant in the beginning of this chapter…*yeah.*

From Albania, With Love

That same night we went back to his room. I loved his bed – not in a sexual way. Chill.

It was technically two beds pushed together and he had the fluffiest covers ever. Added plus – the window was right across the bed and I love a cold room when I sleep. I was laying there for a moment and he joined me as we started talking about my post grad plans (nonexistent, by the way).

You know when you see scenes in movies like this?

A girl and a guy laying on a bed, talking about real stuff and suddenly they turn to each other and gaze into each other's eyes longingly right before a gentle kiss is shared.

Well, that's what happened...except for the kiss. Instead, when we stopped talking and he stared at me he said...

"You know what I can see?"

My heart stopped for a second, thinking he would say some shit like – I see the way your brown eyes aren't really brown because they change color in the light.

Romantic books...man, they set you up for some major disappointment.

"I can see the cracks in your foundation."

What the fuck is going on? Did I just step into some sort of alternate universe?

He didn't mean my foundation as in my past and it wasn't some sort of beautiful metaphor about me. He literally meant the foundation on my face. The foundation I used to hide my rosacea. The foundation I had put on 16 hours ago.

Of course, it would fucking crack. I don't have a make-up team in the morning beautifying me.

Red flag #5.

He started reminding me of my father. Pointing out my flaws instead of complimenting me on the positive aspects of my character.

Trust me, I know my flaws, I don't need the people around me pointing them out.

Have you ever stopped and thought about when you fell in love with someone?

There is always a split-second moment in which you realize you are screwed because you love this person and believe me, it's much worse when you don't know how they feel about you.

The last week of school is usually award season for on campus organizations and the resident advisors. When a person wins an award, they usually gather the people closest to that person and tell them so they can make arrangements for the parents to be there. When Roman won two awards, his resident director called me into the office and told me.

I know what you're thinking. Another movie moment.

She is telling me because she sees we are close – maybe he told her something?

Nope. Pay attention.

I was thrilled for him – over the moon. I knew how much these awards meant to him and I knew how much he would love to see his parents there. Again, kids of immigrants soak up moments to make their parents proud so I understood.

Sophie and another girl – let's call her Rose – had known Roman about two years longer than I had, but we were all friends at that point. All of us made sure Roman's parents were there, but Rose loves structure – more than me. So, she texted Roman's sister to ensure our plan was a go and I even offered to drive over an hour and a half to bring his parents there.

That was the moment. The moment Roman heard his name called out as the winner and his parents came out and surprised him. The look of happiness on his face – I never wanted that to fade. Seeing him happy made me happy. That was love, but this isn't the end of the story.

The next weekend we had the IB senior banquet. In true business fashion, we had one last competition. A sort of capstone in which we worked in groups to consult a local business on an issue they faced. If you haven't realized by now, I am a *VERY* competitive person. Every single competitive project we had – my group always came out as number 1.

Lucy, Nicholas and myself had worked all semester on the project and honestly, we just wanted it to be over. We did extremely well at the presentation so our grades were locked, the only thing left were the awards.

I was allowed to bring someone with me to the banquet, so I asked Roman to come with me. It was an important event for me. The last celebration and completion of a long-winded program. Roman said no. He had to go home that weekend. I wasn't upset. I thought he was joking. I thought he would surprise me and show up to support me.

I thought wrong.

Fucking expectations.

I played my disappointment off like a champ. Of course. Still, I caught myself looking over my shoulder most of the time, hoping to see him standing at the door like this was some sort of fucking plot from a young adult novel.

You know what young adult books don't get wrong? Friends.

Nicholas and Lucy kept me preoccupied and we laughed throughout the dinner even though we got second place.

I didn't get any awards that year – my last year. Not for the diverse show I directed. Not for my work in the Multicultural Center on campus.

Not. A. One.

Once again, I was not enough.

Actually, I won't lie, I did win a competition – a photography competition, which had a money prize. I should have been happy, and for a second I was, but it still didn't feel enough of an accomplishment. The projects I had poured my heart into for four years didn't amount to anything in anybody else's eyes, or maybe I was just disappointed nobody showed up for me the way I showed up for them. Roman didn't show up to my photography competition presentation either, by the way. I sure know how to pick them, and *I sure as fuck know how to not stop.*

Roman was going abroad the following semester, but not before he got through the summer as an orientation leader – oh, yeah, he was a sophomore when I was a senior.

I wanted to do something nice for him. Something he could have to comfort him while he was abroad because while I knew he was outgoing, I also knew he was comfortable where he was, and study abroad makes you see things differently.

What did I do?

The only thing someone who is stupidly in love with someone does.

I wrote him 22 open when letters. If you don't know what they are – look it up. You'll see it right under the category "super romantic and ridiculous things a girlfriend does for her boyfriend".

Each letter is for a different occasion. Open when you feel sad. Open when it's raining. Open at the airport. Open when you have a bad day. Open on a specific date. And on and on.

I hand wrote each letter. I included photos of his family and friends. I wrote song lyrics and poems. I put them inside a box I painted myself and on the inside of the box, I scripted a quote:

"If nothing saves us from death, at least may love save us from life."

It's a quote from Pablo Neruda, one of the best poets to ever live.

If that doesn't scream "I'm in love with you" I don't know what ever fucking could. I told you I am a romantic.

I didn't want to take my chances. I had it all planned. I would give this great speech about how I felt about him, and give him the box, and tell him I only want him to be happy and blah blah blah.

When I got to his room, he was with a friend who didn't intend on leaving any time soon. Fate. She throws hints your way all the time, but I didn't want to listen.

When the friend went to the bathroom, I realized it was then or never. I didn't make a big speech. I didn't even tell him I loved him. I just gave him the box and hoped he could understand.

"This is the nicest thing anybody has ever done for me."

That's what he said, and then we hugged. That was it.

Under whelmed?

Yeah, I know. Me too.

Here is where we pause.

To some of you Roman may seem normal, like he didn't do anything wrong. I should have told him, instead of assume that he liked me because we spent time together, or because we slept in the same bed a few nights, or because he was thrilled when his mom liked me, or because we talked about the future.

You're right, but it doesn't matter, because a month after I graduated Roman got a girlfriend. I never liked her and it wasn't because he was dating her. It was just my vibe. They remained exclusive when he went abroad, but when she went abroad the following semester, she wasn't sure about the exclusive thing.

Ohh...wait, my sixth sense is tingling.

That's right. She was a selfish bitch, but don't worry – they deserved each other after all. Honestly though, I am being a bit harsh – senior year of college is rough. Everybody is really trying to figure things out and maybe she was just unsure of what she wanted – Roman could be a bit too much – almost as if he just wanted a perfect relationship just because it would impress people or it's what they expected of him.

How was I dealing with the news?

I did not turn into some crazed person, if that's what you're thinking. Roman was my best friend before any other feelings developed. I truly imagined us growing up together. Having families and our kids hanging out – if we had kids. It was a lifelong friendship. I was sure and I give 110%, remember?

So why the hostile chapter title?

It was March the last time I saw Roman. 2 years ago. At a funeral.

Seems fitting now.

It's strange really. How you can go from seeing someone every single day to not a single day in two years.

How you can know so much about someone, but the moment they aren't around, you forget all the details, even down to the sound of their voice. If you don't understand, let me explain.

Sophie, Rose and I drove up to our university one day to have brunch with Roman when he had begun his senior year. It was around the same time I had begun writing my manuscript – obviously not this one – but, one we will get too. I was excited and really loving the fact that I had a story in my head and one that I wanted to share with the world. Sophie already knew – she loves reading books. I decided to share the news with the table.

"So, what? Am I in your book?" Roman laughed.

Did anybody else just cringe, because I did. Word of advice to everybody out there:

If your friend ever tells you they are writing a book, don't ever fucking ask if you are in it. Literally pick any other question or maybe just show your support and excitement. I know, not everybody is serious when they say that they are writing a book, but he should have known. He should have known me. I was never the girl to do projects for fun or waste my time. It was my dream, my passion and this person I had revered – I had been in love with, just laughed at me. And, as crazy as this sounds, I didn't hold it against him. I knew not many people would think I was serious or dedicated to my dream and that wasn't my problem.

I was no longer in love with him at this point, by the way. I still loved him, but I was not *in love* with him.

From Albania, With Love

I saw them together once. Roman and his girlfriend. She didn't seem very touchy feely, but he seemed crazy over her, and the emotion that rushed through me at that time made me realize my love for him had evaporated. I wanted him to be happy, even if his happiness was someone else.

That's the difference between love and in love.

After brunch, we headed back to his dorm room and he expressed his confusion about his girlfriend. He wasn't sure about their relationship, but he wanted her to be happy. His doubt was fear. He was afraid to break up with her because he was afraid of what people would say.

They had become the golden couple on campus.

Sort of like that couple who is super involved in the student body and student leadership. Everybody loved them and thought they were the cutest couple ever.

Still, I wanted him to be happy and I thought maybe if I tell him how I felt about him – he will understand love and understand that when you love someone it doesn't necessarily mean you are in love with them.

For his own good, I told him about my past feelings for him.

I bet you are wondering how he reacted…there was nothing. Not a single spec of surprise on his face and I know you are going to say well obviously, – you did all that shit for him.

"I knew you had a thing for me."
Those were his words.

Once again, I internalized, but really this is what I wanted to say.

A thing? Are you fucking kidding me?

You knew all that time and you didn't say shit? You dragged me along with your nice words and suggestive looks when you knew. You kept a hook on me because you liked the attention, even though you pretend like you aren't an attention whore – you liked it when I did nice things for you, like drive eight fucking hours to pick up your favorite cake for your going away party, and write you letters, and skype with you when you felt sad while you were abroad, and engrave a watch to send to you for your birthday in Spain, and believe in your dreams before you even knew what they were, but instead you pretend nobody does anything for you because you like to play the victim? You are a childish, selfish bastard.

I didn't say any of those things because it was all on me. I lost myself.

The real me hates games. The real me likes communication. The real me likes when people are upfront. The real me would have cut that friendship off the moment you didn't have my back. The real me would have cussed you out at brunch when you laughed at my dreams because I believed in yours before you even believed in yourself.

I have a process when dealing with ending a relationship – friendship or otherwise. I sit down and think about the span of the relationship. Everything I did and the other party did. If there has been distance, I look at my effort. Have I done everything I could do to save this relationship?

Now, this limit is endless, there is always something more to do, but I find comfort in the future. If, 15 years, down the line, I am thinking about that person and I am still content with myself about my efforts, then there is nothing to do but move on.

We actually continued talking after that day – Roman and I. Here and there. We were both busy, but in my mind things were different. He texted me wishing me a happy birthday on January 1st of last year and I didn't answer.

Before you jump down my throat, let me remind you that my birthday is on March 1st.

What was left of us wasn't enough, and I finally decided that I was enough.

Lesson of the Chapter

Follow your heart, but listen to your gut.

CHAPTER 19

Early Acceptance, Late Rejection

If you ask a scholar, they will tell you fear is defined as a distressing emotion aroused by impending danger, evil, pain, etc., whether the threat is real or imagined; the feeling or condition of being afraid.

If you go on Pinterest, they will give you a splendid assortment of motivational posters about overcoming your fear and going after what you want.

If you go on Google, they will give you the definition of the word, Fear the 1996 movie, a New York Times review of books, and a link to a TED talk about fear.

If you go on YouTube, they will give you options of different motivational and scholarly videos of fear, how it works, and how you can make it go away.

If you ask me, I will tell you that fear is simply created in our minds when we don't have reassurance of the future. Some people may be okay with that, but most aren't.

Ask anybody sitting close to you – what is your biggest fear?

Dying. Never falling in love. My family dying. Being out of a job.

Future tense. All things which have not occurred.

If you asked any college senior that question, their answer would be graduating without a job. I can guarantee it, because that was my biggest fear. Crossing the stage at graduation without a job secured, without a plan.

And I did. I faced my fear – with or without wanting too.

Now, I know I briefly touched up on how I wanted my life to look post grad. Fabulous marketing job, amazing friends, Sex and the City type life, parties every Friday, and brunch every Sunday. Not too much to ask for, right?

Apparently, fate thought so.

Spring semester, senior year, I took a Writing Fiction course – you remember, the one Roman convinced me to skip one time. The professor was one of those you see in movies who definitely has interesting stories from their past which they like to use to make a difference in class. They make the students think.

Most of the kids in the class did not give a shit. It was just an elective they were taking – probably the "easiest" one, according to them.

We did a lot of short story analysis. I don't like short stories. What are you? A poem, a long essay, or a book? It's a very short amount of time to develop characters or have a plot which draws people in. The class made me appreciate that. Other writers have 300+ pages to make a point, draw the reader in and make a lasting impression and short story authors only have a few pages.

I still don't like short stories, but I can appreciate the artistry.

One day, we were reading a short story about honesty and truth. The character was stuck in some sort of a drug deal gone wrong, but it was totally unlike him to be caught up in the mess. Somehow, the analysis drifted into career paths and our professor told us that no matter what career we go into – we will always tell some sort of lie.

I disagreed. Of course. Did you expect anything less?

When I told him I wanted to go into advertising – he started laughing and said that I would basically be selling lies for a living. That's what I wanted to do. I wanted to create ads and come up with fabulous new ideas. I didn't see myself anywhere else in the business world, but on the creative side and I had no option but to be in the business world.

Like some sort of messed up hero, I wanted to use my position in advertising to help spread a positive message. I had a real chance to shift the system and make a difference.

Apparently, the system liked right where it was.

I had started applying to jobs in spring semester, but honestly, I didn't try very hard. With trying to pass all my classes, to completing my final IB program project, to dealing with the problems of first love – I was caught up and faced my fears. I graduated without a job.

The world didn't end. I was still alive. Everything was fine, except for the guilt.

Immigrant Child Syndrome – I graduated without something to show for it besides an expensive piece of paper.

I had to get to work and I did.

From Albania, With Love

You know how regret can eat away at you? One single moment can remain in your mind for eternity. For me, it was the moment I ripped up the paperwork to transfer majors to English and graduate with a Bachelors in Arts instead of Science, because every single time I applied to a job, I felt like my insides were being ripped out.

Do you know what creative jobs require?

A Bachelor's in Arts.

I had to compensate for what I didn't have. I made a website – designed it myself and I included all the photography I had done over my college years (I loved photography). All my Photoshop work, print ads I had completed in my Advertising classes, and even the ads I had created myself as examples of my talent. I figured a kid with a business degree, self-taught skills of photography and Photoshop, a fresh outlook on the world, an understanding of business, and the ability to speak three languages would get someone's attention.

Once again, I thought wrong.

187 applications.

187 personalized cover letters.

100 rejections.

86 no replies.

1 interview.

Now, you know I don't like math, but even I know, those numbers are depressing as fuck.

The worst part?

The one interview I got was to be a marketing associate at an accounting firm. Which basically meant you get people's coffees and print already formulated, plain and ugly flyers and pamphlets for conferences. That wasn't even the worst part.

They misspelled my name on the rejection letter.

I mean for fuck's sake – it's literally staring at you right in the face. Their rejection was – "we found a better candidate".

Oh, did you now?

To say I was frustrated is an understatement. My life had become a path of guilt and irony. I had received a $200,000 piece of paper to get a job and impress people, but all the jobs required a different piece of paper which I could have had, if I wasn't so concerned with impressing people.

Nothing was working so, like I am now – I wrote a most honest cover letter to my dream advertising firm in Boston. I will not say which firm, but it is to the marketing world like what Ropes & Grey is to the law world.

My gift to you:

Dear Hiring Manager,

I am a recent graduate of Bryant University with a Bachelors in International Business and Marketing and a minor in Professional and Creative Writing. I am extremely interested in establishing a career with X Firm in the marketing field, specifically consulting, digital media, print media, branding, design and advertising but you already know that by now because I guess I wouldn't be applying to this position if I wasn't interested and I think my previous application to your firm sort of gives me away. Besides the point, I believe that the open position of Associate Social Content Solutions is a perfect fit for my skill set, passion and drive to constantly improve and learn.

Now, I guess this is the part of the cover letter when I tell you how awesome I am and how I had all these great experiences that make me qualified for the position but after writing 139 cover letters it all gets to be a little repetitive and since I have wanted to work for X Firm since I finally got my life together and discovered what I wanted to do with my life and I am a firm believer in honesty, I am going to just straight up tell you why I should be considered for this position the only way I know how; by being myself so here goes.

Whoever is reading this is probably shocked at this point that they are not reading some well written and eloquently formatted cover letter, if my cover letter even makes it to somebody's hands to read, but like I said before I will try to be as honest as I can be and tell you a little about myself since I already know so much about X firm; it's only polite you knew a little about me. I was born in Albania, and yes, I speak fluent Albanian and let me tell you it comes in handy sometimes. I followed in my sister's footsteps and went to Bryant University for International Business and Marketing. I can sit here and tell you it's an amazing school and that I had a blast but I promised to be honest. While I did have a great time and meet some amazing people, my

*educational purposes there were not fulfilled and the
university is not to blame, my fear is to blame. Fear of the
unknown, fear that I wasn't good enough to transfer to an
art/design school, fear of my parents being disappointed and
most importantly fear that I would realize I was good enough
but I would never achieve my dreams because let me tell you,
doubt is the root of all failure and I had a lot of doubt.*

*Anyways, let's move away from all the negativity,
shall we? So, sophomore year I realized I wanted to be in the
business of creating life, and not in a creepy GYNO kind of
way, but creating something that inspired people. Capturing
life in movement and designing ideas that did not yet exist
and then I ran into a wall with my recent epiphany. I was at a
heavily business driven school. I am talking classes such as
these: Computer Information Systems, Microeconomics,
Multinational Finance, International Accounting and many
other that make some people in the design world quiver with
fear and others fall asleep with boredom. However, I did take
some classes that pertained to my interests: International
Marketing, Advertising Management and Writing for
Publication but if you notice the list of less preferred classes
is longer and I can even list more. The classes I enjoyed are
listed above and that is the end of that list. I looked at other
avenues and got an internship with the Chafee Center for
International Business as an International Marketing
Researcher and Event Planner. It was a great experience and
I actually did learn a lot about international markets and*

different industries but again there was no creative license or creative projects I could work on.

Finally, I got into photography and my Canon Rebel was my saving grace. I could now photograph anything and create whatever I desired. Turns out, not to toot my own horn, I was pretty good at photography and as a result student organizations hired me to photograph their events and like any normal business mind would think, the people who hired me automatically thought I could do any and everything design and photography related job since you know, apparently, we all fall under the same sector of business and industry.

Whether I liked it or not, I took the jobs because, hey I was a poor college student getting paid $100 for a 4 hour event with editing of those 600+ pictures I just took at that event. The problem was I didn't know that difference between contrast and composition or anything to be completely honest. I was just good at capturing people and emotions and angles in a photo, how was I support to work the million and one buttons Photoshop decided to create? Well, my friend, the internet is a wonderful place for stupid viral videos, for watching Beyoncé shut it down at the VMAs, for ordering books on Chegg or for checking out the latest Buzz Feed article, which I hope I don't become after this cover letter. My personal favorite thing about the internet is the people, specifically the people who upload stupid friendly how to use adobe videos. I sat there for hours and days learning from these videos what would take a normal person a whole *semester or even a whole four years with a certified professor to learn. Now, I am not saying I am better than those people, they just had a little less fear than be about attending an art school. When I would get caught up on something, how to do something on Photoshop, I would just look it up on Google and with that I created 8 advertising campaigns for both student organizations and school work. My favorite part of the whole journey was people's faces when you showed them your finished product; it was like the Christmas present they had been waiting for all year. They would be so excited and impressed and in the back of my mind I kept thinking; if only you knew how much time I spent on that perfectly lined text on that poster you are now running your hands over.*

And just like that, I became the most famous creative designer to ever exist.... No, I was just joking but wouldn't that be a happy ending to my long cover letter and story. A triumphant victory for the girl who had a rough start and knew nothing about the industry or art! Sounds like a book or Hollywood movie, doesn't it? I hate to be the bearer of bad news but those happy ending stories haven't actually ended, it was just the quick chapter that came to a conclusion and that is more likely story. Despite my harsh honesty in this cover letter, I am extremely hard working and want nothing more than to finally be able to show my creativity to the world even if it's just a world made up of 2 people. I guess what I am trying to say is this cover letter is short compared to what I have had to go through to actually get to figure out what my life purpose is and have the courage to pursue that dream.

*Since this position is "Associate" level I figure I can learn
what I was never able to while at school and maybe you can
learn a little something from me; after all I can bring that
25% business, 75% creative brain on to the team.*

*I don't expect you to believe that I am actually worth
an interview or the position because I wrote a sassy cover
letter so please take a look at myself built website at
migenadulaj.com. I hope X Firm can be the start to my new
chapter and lucky number 140 so I look forward to hearing
for you!*

> *Sincerely,*
> *Migena Dulaj*

Life path, yeah right…. *AND* damn, that was a lot of
run on sentences, and horrible grammar.

You know what that got me?

You guessed it…nothing. Well, actually I did get a
personalize rejection instead of a computer animated thanks,
but no thanks.

Still… no job.

When I was in college I worked at this International
Business Center. Local companies would come and seek
advice on different aspects of trading internationally and the
team of people who worked there helped them out – with the
assistance of student workers.

I sort of did it all while I worked there; secretary,
assistant, marketing researcher, AV tech, and presentation
editing.

In the midst of my job draught, one of the older gentlemen, who worked there, reached out to me. A company in Rhode Island specializing in home décor design and production was looking for a marketing assistant.

Hallelujah!

A home décor company and marketing – those were two of my favorite things.

I nailed my interview, considering I didn't have very much practice, but if going to business school and having to complete at least one presentation a month taught me anything – it was to sell anything even if it was bullshit, and you had no idea what you were talking about.

When I got the job, I was ecstatic, but still there was a gut feeling in my stomach. I knew I should have been genuinely thrilled, especially since I was about to begin repayment on my hefty college loans, but there was just something there blocking natural happiness.

What was my lesson last chapter?

Ohh... yeah, I remember, but that still doesn't mean I take my own advice.

Lesson of the Chapter

Fear is a copping mechanism your mind creates when faced with uncertainty.

CHAPTER 20

4,449 Miles

They claim that grief has seven stages; shock, denial, anger, bargaining, depression, testing, and acceptance. It's all great in theory – you move along the stages of grief until you can feel your life return to normal. The only thing they don't include is a time line.

I only felt one of those seven stages.

After my job hunting episode, I started working at the home décor company, 55 miles away from my house. It was quite a hike, but it was a job.

I don't know if you have figured this out by now, but I don't like to sit still. I don't like doing nothing and that was exactly what the job turned out to be. An advertised grand marketing job with opportunities for me to expand and use my creative talents turned out to be just sitting at a desk, answering emails, printing standard flyers, and trying to find something to fill my time with.

This piece that I am now writing, I actually began writing in that horrid French class in college with that awful TA, who did nothing but talk about sex and death. On top of all her weird writing topics, the Wi-Fi was crappy and we were not allowed to have our laptops so, to good old pen and paper I went. My piece was nowhere near as honest as this, but I was feeling a bit inspired after speaking with my writing professor, who wanted me to tell my story. I wanted to see if there was anything there.

I wrote two paragraphs and I didn't touch the idea until three years later, when I had my most wonderful job in Rhode Island. There was something about the people I worked with - their simplicity and narrowmindedness that got me thinking about life. I had achieved what I thought was my life goal of working in an office and I was losing my mind.

It only took about three days for me to realize that that life wasn't for me.

I couldn't write how I honestly felt, because God forbid people read it, so I translated it into a work of fiction. I wanted people to know about my background, my influences, and what young immigrants go through in life. I started a very rough draft of what I now have sitting on my desk and staring at me every time I work.

If we want to get technical, I started writing stories in middle school. In college after I was done with school work and sometimes even before, I would take characters that already existed, from movie or books, and I would rewrite a different story – like fanfiction, but without all the weird sex stuff. I recently did the math on those stories I wrote in college, and turns out I wrote 316,000 words in total. Book pages – that's probably around 1,000 pages.

Damn. I really don't shut up sometimes.

At the time, I only wrote two chapters of that manuscript which I am now trying to desperately get published. Why?

From Albania, With Love

I had just arrived at work the morning of January 5th, 2015. It was freezing that morning so I had turned my car heat all the way up. It was so loud, I almost didn't hear my phone obnoxiously ringing. It was my mom, which wasn't rare as she sometimes called to make sure I got to work okay, but she wasn't calling to make sure I was okay. She was calling to let me know she wasn't okay.

My grandma died.

I wasn't shocked. I wasn't alarmed. I wasn't anything.

Just numb.

Keeping in my true fashion, I jumped into action. I drove home after telling my boss I was going to be out for the week, and I booked our tickets to go home. Me, my sister and my mom.

$6,000.00

Turns out, death is expensive too.

Two hours later, we got on a flight heading to Milan. Then a flight to Tirana. Our uncle met us there and drove us home to Fier.

You know when I told you I don't know what celebrities go through when they are hounded by the media? Well, I sort of lied.

My uncle navigated the streets of Fier well and when we got to the street I grew up on – the street with the house I used to love so much, people crowded the car, like we were the Obamas landing in the US after being away for a while. There were no cameras, but their eyes were just the same.

When we stepped out of the car, I don't think I have ever seen that many people I didn't recognize, looking at me like I was the show. Don't understand?

Well, we had arrived from America – the land of the free and wealthy, so we were like a specimen to them, and stepping inside the house was not any better. I hadn't been back in ten years, so even family looked like strangers, let alone the crowds of people in the house. You would think being surrounded by alive people would make me feel comfortable, but you would think wrong.

Fier, Albania has the approximate weather of Santa Monica, California. Beautifully sunny and warm most of the year. Even when it rains, it's warm, but I had never felt a colder air rip through Fier than when I stepped into that house. The orange trees still had fruit on them, but I had never seen them so dull. The vibrant green colored door seemed like the color of a dreary forest just before night fall. The warm cinnamon air the house was replaced by the smell of candle wax burning. Everything just seemed like it was missing something.

Stepping into the living room was like stepping into a different world.

You see, in Albania death is done a little differently. The wake – if you can even call it that – is before the funeral and it's done at the person's home, not a wake house. I was not aware of this fact, so when I walked into the living room and saw my grandma's body just resting there, I don't really know what my face looked like, but my nails dug into my palms so badly that I later discovered bloody half-moon shapes on my skin. I realized why they made me sit in the kitchen when my grandpa died.

My mom was a mess and my sister cried on the plane, in the car and when we walked into the living room. I had not felt a single tear down my cheek. I couldn't afford it. I had to be there for my mom, who was crying over my grandma's body.

My aunt had the absurd idea for me to kneel over the body and give my grandma a kiss on the cheek. I don't think anybody has ever lost it at a funeral, but I almost did. I looked at her like she had lost her fucking mind and she backed off.

That body was not my grandma. It was not the woman who raised me. It was not the woman who cooked for me. It was not the woman who believed in me so blindly and without reason. It was not the woman who told me to tell Roman to fuck off after I told her things didn't work out. It was not the woman who made inappropriate jokes in the most inopportune times. It was not the woman who made me feel like I was enough....

.

.

Sorry guys, this is just a lot.

Albanians have this awful saying when someone is driving super slow.

"Why are you driving like you are going to a funeral?"

I never understood the expression, but I did after we drove to the cemetery. People were walking past the car faster than the cars were driving. It was slow motion torture.

I didn't attend very many sports games in college, but my freshman year in college – my sister got me seats to the Celtics game. Two seats above courtside type of seats. Amazing. I have never seen that many people in one place before. I know, I have some pretty weird observations, but it felt nice. We were all cheering for our home team – there was a sense of unity.

Standing at the top of the hill, where my grandpa was buried, as we prepped to bury my grandma, I felt like I had never seen that many people in my life before. There must have been at least 500 people there and my aunts were secretly thrilled. You see, even death is just another occasion to show off in Albania. The more people show up to your funeral, the more respected you are thought to be.

I didn't care.

My eyes were stuck on the men unearthing my grandpa so they could be buried together. Oh yeah, things in Albania were still not as high tech as the United States. Where you have hydraulics and fancy carpets at funerals, Albania has two men in the grave helping lower the coffin down. The open coffin, by the way – they close it when the person is 6 feet under.

I refused to see my grandma lowered into the earth, so I looked up to see the sea of people and still, I have never felt that alone in my entire life.

198

From Albania, With Love

Death is funny in a way. It's like when you see the expiration date on a box of cookies and you suddenly remember how delicious they are.

I couldn't get it out of my head as much as I tried to look away. The memory of my grandma being lowered into the ground. All these images kept flashing in my head of where my life was and how absolutely none of it was what I wanted. I wasn't happy, and in death, that's all that matters. Nobody remembers how many likes you got on a photo; how impressive you were to other people; how much money you made; what people thought of you.

Are you happy?

That's all.

In death, there is nothing but regret.

The only thing I could think about on the treacherous plane ride back was my writing. I had not been writing as quick as I wanted to, because I was afraid of people not liking it, people not caring, people not listening. I was stuck in a box of self-doubt and second guessing. I was writing what I thought people would want to read, instead of writing what they needed to read – what my heart was telling me to write.

That fitting in thing? It's a major bitch.

After an awful week of greeting people, pretending like I remembered them even though I didn't give a shit, being in my home country, and staring death in the face, surprisingly I had a renewed sense of nationalism. I wanted to tell Albania's story and maybe even my own a little bit.

To me, the absolute worse part about being an immigrant, is not knowing where you belong. As I told you it always goes back to fitting in. When you arrive to the US, you try and convert – become an American. When you go home, you are too far gone – they claim you have forgotten your Albanian roots. So, you bring them back with you, to America, but America wants nothing to do with your Albanian nationalism. You are now too Albanian, too foreign. You don't belong.

So who even are you?

Believe me it's an identity crisis every immigrant endures and it deserved a story – or so I thought. I finally believed my crazy professor who claimed I had a story to tell. So, why did it take me close to a year to even jot down the first few sentences?

The seven stages of grief. Only one found me and hasn't left me.

Depression.

Lesson of the Chapter

Do things that make you happy without a second thought.

CHAPTER 21

7,300 Hours

I cried a lot as a baby, or so I've been told. My sister wasn't any better, but apparently, I didn't stop no matter the time of day. My mom's downstairs neighbor told her that if she had another kid, then he would move. He was a straight up asshole, if you ask me.

Right around the nine-month mark, the crying got worse, so my mom went to the hospital. They admitted me since I had a high fever and injected me with whatever medicine they saw fit to bring down the fever.

Remember when I told you Albania still is not as advanced as the US in medicine?

The doctors did all they could with what they had, but I wasn't responding – the fever remained and I got worse, so they told my mom to expect not to bring me home because I would more than likely die.

Brutal honesty.

One of the many things people stereotype Albanians to do and be, one of them is sort of true.

Black magic.

Okay, chill. We aren't witches or anything, but we do have a varied number of superstitions, and belief that certain people can foresee things, or even place a sort of curse on someone. I don't really believe in superstitions as most of them are just something someone made up a long time ago and it got passed down like a bad game of telephone. That being said, I am not necessarily thrilled if a black cat crosses my path.

I do believe there are some people who can foresee the future, but I don't think they are sham fortune tellers who, for a cheap rate of $19.99 a minute, will tell you who you will marry and how many kids you will have.

My family takes it to a new level.

One time my cousin got really sick – something to do with his stomach, which has never been a problem for anybody in the family, and my grandma (on my dad's side) insisted that he had stepped into a curse or fate meant for someone else.

Explain that shit to me.

Here's a logical explanation: sometimes, bad things happen to good people.

My mom is a believer like my family, so when nothing was working, she went a different way.

There was an old lady from a nearby village who was considered a healer or fortune teller of some sort. The only really good name I can give her is a prophet. She couldn't tell you what was going to happen, or the future, but she could sense or feel or see the path ahead.

They brought the old lady to the hospital. She didn't even hold me or touch me – she saw me through a glass window and she turned to my mom and said,

"Take her home. She is meant for so much more."

Now, let me remind you, the tubes and medicine I was connected to at the hospital were basically keeping me alive, but without any doubt in her mind, my mom believed the woman and checked me out against medical advice.

I told you...my family believes in that stuff, *A LOT*.

Not even two days later, I was back to normal – like nothing had ever happen, like doctors didn't tell my mom I was going to die.

Brujería.

Even though my mom told me that story all the time, I was still skeptical of the whole system my family believed in. Surprisingly, I like facts and reality – things I can see and touch.

Here's the reality.

Those two chapters I wrote before my grandma passed, remained at the length and exact word count for nine months.

I told you, I am not a crier. Maybe I had gotten it all out when I was a baby, but I didn't see a point. You cry and then what? Your problems remain the same – so, I never bothered. I only cried once in the whole week, and when we flew back, I was ready to get to work – taking care of my mom, working my jobs, and writing the story I had always wanted to write.

For about two weeks, my plan worked.

On a not so special night in February, I woke up at 1:30AM and I just stared at everything in the darkness of my room. I didn't have a nightmare, I didn't remember a bad memory, but I just sat there. My back was flushed against the cold wall, next to the window and I felt a drop on my hand. I hadn't realized I had started crying, and I didn't know why I was feeling so sad, but an overwhelming feeling of death surrounded me.

I can't formulate the right words to describe the feeling to you, but I thought I was going to die. I had a feeling. A sense that if I went back to bed, I would not wake up in the morning.

I told you, I don't scare easy, but that night, I was terrified, and I was alone.

I couldn't wake my parents or my sister up, because I was convinced they would think I had lost my mind, which I sort of felt I had.

I didn't sleep that night. I just sat and stared.

I would love nothing more than to tell you it was just an episode, because I was sad about my grandma, but it only got worse.

Every morning before work or anytime I left the house, I would take ten minutes and look at everything in my room and the house. I would run my fingers over everything in my room so I could remember every sensation, before I died. I thought that every time I left the house, I would get into an accident and die. I would avoid public transportation because someone might have some sort of rare disease that I would get and die.

I would see signs of my impending death everywhere.

From Albania, With Love

A crow passing over my car just before I got on the road meant I would die. When I was filling my car with gas and the dollar amount stopped on my age then I would die. If I slept at night, I would not wake up in the morning. If I was driving and my eyes randomly looked at the streets and I saw a funeral home, it meant I was going to die. On the off chance that I watched a movie or TV show and a character died that meant I would die.

My mind felt so weak and my body wasn't doing any better.

I had a doctor's appointment and he asked me how I was doing. I told him I was a little sad about my grandma, but the words, "I'm depressed and I think I am going to die" never slipped from my lips. Yes, he could have helped me and he could have prescribed medication, but I come from a culture in which mental illness doesn't exist.

I wasn't depressed, I was just sad.

I wasn't losing my mind, I was just stressed.

My whole life, I thought people used depression as an excuse. They were just sad and they needed to get over it. That's what I was taught to believe – just like when someone was about to commit suicide, my family said that she had lost her mind and just needed to go find it. There was nothing physically wrong with her, so she was fine.

Maybe this was my karma. A way to teach me a lesson that depression is not just being sad. Yes, there are different stages of depression, but nothing hurts more than having to hide it because you think the people who are supposed to love you unconditionally are going to hate you, because you think that you have lost your mind, because you think there is something wrong with you, because you think you are being weak after holding it together for so fucking long.

I know the stigma is that usually people who are depressed are also suicidal, but trust me that's not the case. I was terrified of dying because I thought it was going to happen at any moment and I wasn't ready to go.

Everybody is different. Everybody handles things differently.

Depression isn't always crying your mascara away or listening to sad songs. Sometimes it's just not wanting to talk to anybody for days, but being sad about the fact that there is nobody around you. Sometimes depression is not having an appetite for anything even though you can't remember the last time you ate and being sad that not even your favorite dish is appealing. Sometimes it's going to dinner with your family and being sad for no reason at all and having to pretend like you are enjoying yourself. Sometimes depression doesn't hit you at 3AM, it hits you at 3PM when everybody else is fine and you are far from it. Most times it's keeping it all inside because you don't want the people you love to look at you like you are broken or weak. It's the frustrating feeling of wanting nothing but just to be happy even though you are surrounded by gray clouds.

Almost every single time, depression is an empty feeling like your chest is hollow and your ribs are echoing against nothing, but your bones are radiating with pain. There is not a single thing anybody can say or do to fill the space or ease the pain.

You can feel yourself drowning even though you know how to swim.

I spent 7,300 hours thinking I was going to die at any given minute, and I didn't know when it would end. I still went to work. I still lived my life. I still carried on, but nothing I did could get my mind away from the places it was choosing to go. There was nothing I could do to make it go away.

I wish I could tell you that I have some sort of miracle pill to make those bad thoughts go away. Like, I found a way to stop thinking I was going to die.

Isn't that the way it always happens in movies or books?

Something happens one day or a character has a life changing conversation with a friend and suddenly the plot shifts. That's the problem with fiction. We use it to escape our life, but somewhere along the way – we expect our life to be like that made up world we use to escape.

I can't remember the day I stopped thinking I was going to die. It wasn't as much me thinking that I wasn't going to die as it was me accepting that I was in fact going to die, but whether I worried about it or not, would not make it come any faster or slower.

The day I accepted death, I also forgot about everybody else. If I was going to die, I didn't really give a fuck about people's opinions, even the opinions of those closest to me. I was my own person and writing became my outlet.

If you haven't realized by now that this is a collection of stories about fitting in and finding your voice – we are reading different stories. Without realizing it, all my life, I had been trying to fit in and be who everybody wanted me to be.

I tried to be American. I tried to remain Albanian. I tried to make people proud. I went to a school I didn't really want to go to. I finished a major I wasn't interested in. I hung out with people who did not reflect who I wanted to become. I always made sure others were happy. I even change the way my name is supposed to be pronounced so that I could belong somewhere.

It was all fine, until it wasn't. Until I realized that I hadn't really been happy. I had just internalized. I had been strong, mature, and celebrated among the Albanian community as a shining example of a daughter. Never got in trouble, went to a great school, worked at a great job in an office, and never caused any scandals for my parents.

It wasn't enough. It wasn't me.

When I would sit down and write, nothing else existed for me. The hurt, the pain, the depression, the people, the guilt – nothing was there but my characters and the worlds I was building. I didn't need to fit in anywhere in my novel. Nobody could alter it or take it away from me. It was a world I belonged in because I created it.

I was never suicidal, but writing saved my life.

Remember when I told you guys – all the way back, in the prelude – that trying to fit in is a danger to your health? Well, it took me thinking I was going to die for 304 days straight to realize that.

Little by little, minute by minute, day by day and week by week, my fear of dying went away and with it, it took my life long desire to make everybody proud of me.

I simply needed me to be proud of me.

Sounds great, right?

So, why did I say depression found me and hasn't left me?

Because, nobody ever talks about the dark side of writing and publishing, but that's what I'm here for.

Lesson of the Chapter
Make yourself proud first.

CHAPTER 22

Three Jobs, Three Months, One Manuscript

You have probably figured out by now that there are not many things which irk me. I have a mountainous amount of patience, because there are other things on my mind, but still every once in a while, I am reminded of things which bother me.

Things that irk me:

People wearing sunglasses indoors, unnecessarily bitchy people, racists, not having my iced coffee in the morning, bullies, societal standards in reference to creative professions, Whole Foods parking lots, and people blaming time for not achieving something.

There are probably other things on that list, but just remember that last one. It's key.

If you ask two authors about their writing method and process, I can guarantee their answers will be different. Specifically, what is in the background while they write. Some like silence. Some like music. Some like TV. You get the idea.

I am not the silent type. I love to listen to music and the worse question anybody can ask me is what is your favorite type/genre because I literally listen to it all, and I mean ALL. Pop, hip hop, rock, reggaeton, k-pop, rap, classical, r&b, contemporary, tech. My problem is I get easily bored and annoyed some days, so I found something else.

YouTube. No, I didn't just discover YouTube, but I did discover some pretty cool motivational videos. I know what you are thinking.

Ugh, those videos where those guys just yell and tell you not to be lazy.

Yeah, there are a few videos like that, but that's not what I listen to.

I discovered a guy named Eddie Pinero. He has a channel on YouTube called Your World Within, and his videos are pretty magnificent. He has a calming voice and he does not shout – even better, it's all his material – not some scene from a motivational sports movie.

Anyway, he has this video in which he talks about the desire to achieve something. It's not a long video – only about four minutes, but here is a little excerpt.

"It's been said that it takes 10,000 hours to perfect your craft. 10,000 hours of walking away from immediate satisfaction to enter this sentence of solitude and dedication to where you weed out mediocrity, to where you carve out your place in history, and if you're waiting for someone to come along and just make that happen for you, it will be a long wait, my friend, because it's your flame and if you don't keep it lit, it will die. That flame can be a fragile thing. Weakness. Doubt. Uncertainty. Failures. They all want to put it out and if you aren't bigger than your body, they will. Trust me, you'll fail. Time and time again. It may not be until your 100th attempt that you may begin to see success, but if you don't have the foresight and persistence to see past the bumps

on the road, you will never know. Nothing good falls into your hands. People will never see your 10,000 hours – they will only see your last 30 seconds."

I had never written a real book before. I knew nothing about the publishing world or how to get published. So, I did my homework. Here's how it goes, kids. *Pay attention.*

First, you write a book. Second, you decide if you will go the traditional publishing route or the self-publishing route. I will not give you positive and negatives of those methods. You should do some homework, but let's assume you go the traditional route. Third, you research agents, because here's a fun fact; major publishing houses don't give a shit if you have the best manuscript on the face of the planet. If you aren't represented by a literary agent, your manuscript will end up in the trash before you can say the word author. Fourth, you query the agents you would like to be represented by.

A query is like an email from hell. It's sort of a cover letter for your book. A two to three paragraph summary of a manuscript which is probably 300+ pages. How in the fuck is that possible? Writing the query was more difficult for me then writing 117,000 words. A query letter is also the first impression an agent has of you, your professionalism, your story, your style of writing, your message. AND, the bitch of it all is they all like to see different things in the letter, so coming up with a general query letter is like trying to fold a fitted sheet. Fucking impossible.

Pause.

Here is where things get complicated and the reason why you are reading this swear filled collection of stories instead of my young adult manuscript.

I am stuck at number four. I don't have an agent. Yet. I'll explain – I promise.

This is what my research shows me will happen after you complete step four of attempting to get published.

Fifth, you sign a contract with your agent. Sixth, depending on how ready your manuscript is, you and your agent prep it and shop it at publishing houses. The better your manuscript, especially in young adult, the more Game of Thrones type fights happen between the publishing houses. Seventh, you sign a deal to get published – YAY!!

Eighth, ninth and tenth, you go back and forth editing with your editor until it's perfect and it goes into production. The rest of the journey depends on your type of book, agent's push, and reader's excitement, but let's focus on step number one for now.

I am not going to give you some sort of motivational speech here about how to write a book and you can do it, and all that bullshit. I told you this is my story and my point of view. So, here is the only advice I will give you.

How do you write a book?

You don't go online and look for resources. You don't go to seminars in which people tell you how to write villain's or other types of characters. You don't look online for some sort of motivational inspiration to write.

213

You put your ass in a chair and you just fucking type.

You want to know why?

Because no two-people read the same book. Just write what is in your heart and someone will connect with it. Notice I didn't say someone will like it?

When you create art, you aren't looking for someone to like it, you are looking to connect to another human.

People don't connect to books because they like or dislike them. They connect to books because they feel like the characters understand them, and what they are going through makes the reader feel less alone. I'm sure executives of publishing houses sitting on their high chair will tell you there is a formula to a successful book. Romance, characters people like, a love story, a dramatic element and so on. Maybe that's true, but none of the best-selling authors you see on bookshelves sat down and came up with a manuscript with elements perfectly concocted to sell.

Nobody sits down to write a book solely because they think it will make them rich. If they do, they seriously have no fucking idea how rough this journey can be.

So, what happened?

I left that marketing assistant job in Rhode Island. It was too much while I was dealing with everything else and honestly, it was a waste of time. It wasn't what I wanted to do. I will spare you the details because if we get into it we will be here all day.

I focused on my writing, but because this is real life – I couldn't just sit at home and write like I was in some sort of movie montage. You know what the real world also has?

Student loan payments.

Fuck.

I knew the office environment wasn't for me so I went into retail. Famous last words. These are stories for another time, but the point of the story is, I was determined and excited about writing my work of fiction. I was just coming down from my awful thoughts about my potential death, so I buried myself in my manuscript. It was my safe space.

Remember in the beginning of this chapter when I told you to pay attention to the fact that I get irked when people use time as an excuse for not achieving something or doing something?

My daily schedule at the time in question:

6:00AM – Wake up

7:00AM – 4:00PM – Job #1

4:30PM – 5:30PM – Shower, eat dinner, and get ready.

6:00PM – 11:00PM – Job #2

11:30PM – 3:30AM – Write my manuscript.

That was my life. Every single day and on weekends I had another job. I finished my manuscript in three months. So, when someone told me, they didn't have time for something, I simply told them to take several fucking seats.

I know what some of you are thinking.

Well, it was your fault. You should have gotten a better paying job and just made it work.

You're right, but I would rather work a million times harder than spiral completely out of control in an office. I happened to care about my mental health.

My point here is, if you want something, you will literally do everything in your power to get it. Nobody gives you time. You have to make time, because sometimes life isn't fair.

Did I wish I went to an arts school? Sure.

Did I wish I started writing seriously earlier in life? Sure.

Would my life be a hell of a lot easier if I had connections? Yep.

Would my life be where I want it to be if I hadn't waited so long to realize what I wanted to do? I don't know.

Do I wish I could go back in time? Sometimes.

When do you know that you have found your passion? When you want something as bad as you want to breathe.

So, what is this book about exactly?

Oh, my God! I'm actually so excited to tell you guys!

Considering this whole honest piece, you are now reading is about my immigration journey, you can imagine my book is also about that. It is exactly based on the Immigrant Diversity Visa we talked about earlier – the one that brought me to the US. I didn't want to go back, I wanted to go forward. I imagined what our world would look like in a couple hundred years from now – with the issues of capitalism, war, the environment, and a potential world war.

Here we go.

The setting of the book is in a world divided into two. The Vatra Republic created after ruin, war and lots of other problems has two Hemispheres; the Vetus Hemisphere, an inspired fascist regime, but friendlier (aka old Albania) & the Novati Hemisphere, a modern (totally off the books) royal monarchy (aka my interpretation of the US).

So, when they first created the republic they did not want to ruin things by rushing. They took time to rebuild and in a meeting of the leaders they came up with a plan to move forward. But how? Both sides thought they had the best government and ideas of the future.

Well, they came up with a model citizen, someone who would do well under any regime, for when they would eventually join the republic into one. They also establish pillars a model citizen of the future should reflect.

The Novati Hemisphere already exemplified lots of these pillars so they offered to host the experiment, and the Vetus Hemisphere offered the citizens, all in an effort to build the future together and without another world war.

Every year, the Republic hosts the Lottery experiment and selects 16 young citizens at random (8 boys, 8 girls) of the Vetus Hemisphere as test subjects to become the model citizens of the future and become part of history or so they say.

The training is modeled after my experience of becoming a citizen in the USA and trying to fit in somewhere based on what people tell you is best for the future. To me, there is no better person that understands that then a teenager – immigrant or not.

And of course, tension and revolution is a must! But seriously, both sides have major issues.

The Vetus Hemisphere has people who want to join the Hemispheres NOW! They don't think it's fair that only a few get the chance to build the future and they think the republic is hiding something. Meanwhile the Novati Hemisphere is dealing with some racist ass people, who want to purify the Hemispheres and destroy the Lottery. They want to remain separate and never join together.

Remind you of a place right now?

Moving on, we find our MC – main character. This poor girl - love her though, even though I put her through hell and back. What are main characters for if not that?

Seventeen-year-old Aleksija (Albanian ass name) lives in the Vetus Hemisphere and because of her dead father's criminal past, she is forced to deal with all the shit. People talk about her, her fate, how she is nothing - real rude shit, man, but Aleksija doesn't care. She is happy with keeping her head down and taking care of her brother. She, unlike the rest of the citizens of the Vetus Hemisphere, does not really care for the Lottery, even though girls whisper about how grand it might be and how they would kill for a chance to see the other Hemisphere and be history makers.

But then, I think you know what is coming next......Aleksija is chosen to partake in the experiment and never return home.

Damn, man. That's cold.

So, she leaves behind her brother and her childhood friend (aka the only person who did not act like a douche when her father broke the law) and heads to the Novati Hemisphere. And it's about to go down like you can't imagine.

You know, the sort of things that happen when there is royalty, scandals, and a republic involved.

Obviously, Aleksija finds out that the Lottery is nothing more than a chance to pit her fellow Vetus Hemisphere citizens against each other, and they already all hate her so things aren't looking good. Each challenge tests her emotionally, physically and mentally, but don't worry she makes friends as she tries to deal with her internalizing ways. Remind you of anybody?

So, why do this at all you ask? Why doesn't she just say, no, I don't want to do this.

Well, the King announces that the winners (male and female) will have their family brought to the Novati Hemisphere as a reward for their incredible sacrifice, and to signal the unity of the republic.

Aleksija gets to work and hopes she can provide a better life for her brother than the one they had back home.

Don't worry people aren't killed off when they are eliminated...this is a friendly Kingdom (sort of), but the fate that awaits them is much worse.

AND, we can't forget the Prince. Ohhh... be still my heart. The Crown Prince of the Novati Hemisphere is not one to play by the rules nor does he necessarily give a shit about what his father, the King, wants or expects from him.

Where is the Queen?

Well you guessed it.....she's dead. The Crown Prince sets his sights on Aleksija and she forces herself to use his popularity to win over the people, but he has a plan of his own. No, they don't fall in love instantly. You know I hate that shit.

Soon enough, Aleksija becomes part of a game of power that has started even before she was born. *(Ouuuu!)*

It gets wild. If any of you have ever seen the show The Royals on E! then just imagine that mixed with Reign on the CW, mixed with a fantasy monarchy and fascist government all wrapped up in one.

Sounds pretty bad ass, right?

I thought so too, but apparently other people didn't.

Lesson of the Chapter

Nobody, but you, is ever really going to know how
much something means to your soul.

CHAPTER 23
The Dark Side

We open this chapter with an Albanian tradition/superstition.

Don't worry, it's not a hex.

I don't know if other families follow this tradition or if it is even still done in Albania, but my whole family participated. I told you I had a shit ton of cousins – my Sailor Moon cousins are just the beginning, and we all were part of the tradition.

When a baby turns one year old the family sits the baby on the floor in front of a few items such as a toy police car, a pen, a pencil, a stethoscope, a protractor and a few other things I can't remember at this point. So, your entire family waits for you, a one year old, to choose an item that will represent your career choice. It's like a romanticized version of a career aptitude test without a realistic basis. A baby is obviously going to pick the shiniest thing. I didn't mind the tradition – I might even make my kids do it, if I have any, but my problem was always the choices presented.

There are probably only six or seven choices because you know, there are only six or seven careers available in life, and they are all traditional careers. I know, I know. If they tried to include all the possible careers, the baby would end up lost in thousands of random objects.

What did I choose you ask?

From Albania, With Love

The pen.

Out of all the shiny colors and loud siren objects, I chose a simple black pen. Fate. She was trying to throw hints since day one, even before I split my head open.

For those of you who don't know – choosing a pen meant I would grow up to be a writer. Ironic as fuck. Fate has a sense of humor after all.

Is this where you are hoping I suddenly tell you after all my hard work and this touching pen story, everything works out perfectly.

Then you haven't been paying attention, but I can't blame you. I expected the same thing.

I thought and still do, that I have an amazing story with some pretty spectacular characters, and the key when going into anything creative is belief. You have to be self-confident. The only problem is sometimes there is a terrifyingly dark side to writing and trying to get published.

I know I am going to sound like a high school student opening her college essay, but Mark Twain once said, "The two most important days in your life are the day you are born and the day you find out why."

I can't really pin point a day when I realized I was put on this earth to write. I realized after I found out that anything that had come before didn't matter. Besides my deep, deep need to fit in, I had never felt like I had a job or something I was working towards that I would feel no regret or have to think twice about doing the rest of my life. I loved doing photography, but it got to a point when I realized I would never want to have it be my career.

I know what some of you might say.

You have only really written professionally for about two years and you only have one story under your belt.

You are right, but I can't describe the feeling. I don't ever see myself doing anything else. I have seen what literature can mean to people and I saw it first-hand what it did for me. I don't think it comes as a surprise when I say I didn't have the best examples in my childhood for freedom, for encouragement to unapologetically be myself, and I know I wasn't alone. I have a voice, and I want to speak for those who can't or don't think they have anything to say, and I want to do it through my characters and my words.

I thought the universe was on my side.

When I first started querying agents, I made an excel spreadsheet. I told you, I like structure. I would jot down agency names, agent name, date, location, and response. I used the internet for a lot of my research as how to go about this. I looked at query examples, read up on agency history, looked over clients they had, and on and on. The only thing I didn't do is research how many agencies I would approximately need to query until I found my agent.

Almost everybody you tell about your writing, tells you one thing only.

"Oh... that's a really tough business."

Tell me something I don't fucking know.

Why not just congratulate them on the fact that they had endurance to finish a manuscript instead of telling them a fact they are well aware of.

I told you a few chapters back that once I make up my mind, it's close to impossible to change it. Let's add another fact to that; I love proving people wrong.

So, I didn't listen to what anybody had to say – I just kept moving forward.

I kept writing. I kept editing. I kept querying. I never took my mind away from my book.

I didn't watch TV for a year. I didn't go out with friends. I didn't go anywhere but my computer to send queries and continue writing. I felt guilty if I went somewhere because I wasn't home writing. I never took a break. When I went to Barnes and Noble or any bookstore, instead of looking at a book to buy it, I flipped to the back and saw who the author's agent was in the acknowledgements section. I built up my website so that when agents clicked on my link they could better understand what I wanted my message to be.

It was obsession at its purest form. I was living, breathing and dying for my story, but still the number of agents queried kept increasing.

I tried a different approach – not necessarily much of an approach, but nevertheless.

I discovered the new, established, and up and coming young adult authors and I followed them on social media. I read up on them to find comfort, like maybe they had also had a hard time finding an agent straight away, but it did not help. It actually hurt.

Jealousy is a strong emotion that, to me, only exists in the human heart when that heart cares. I wouldn't say I was jealous of these authors, but I just kept comparing everything about them to me. Some days I worshiped them and their achievements, other days I hated them because I thought I deserved to be there and most days, I just got discouraged. I know we are supposed to say, I am so happy this person or that person just got a book deal, but I was miserable. It wasn't their fault – obviously, but in my head – it was just another spot gone.

And, believe me – it was not about me. In those rare moments, I just felt like people could relate to my story, my characters and I felt like I was missing my chance to make the world a better place. I felt like I would never get my opportunity to help others by using my voice.

I would see authors at conferences and on tour through their Instagram and Twitter and I would be genuinely happy, because I know how treacherously difficult it is to write a book and connect with people, but I was still jealous and upset.

I didn't want their life – I just didn't want to feel like I was waiting for my life to start.

The rejections were and still are the worse part. They have become second nature, but I never stopped. I did everything perfectly. I never misspelled a last name. I never addressed an email as Dear Agent. I was boarder line creeping on the agents on their social media pages to personalize each letter. I never claimed my book was the next best seller.

I never stopped. On a good day, I would send out at least 10 emails.

For those of you who don't know, most people suggest you send out 10 at a time and wait for answers.

That's the other thing. The waiting.

You send an email out and you wait four to six weeks. In my case, I waited four to six weeks for a rejection, so I would just send out multiple in one week.

About 150 queries in, I was accustomed to rejections. They just rolled off my shoulder. On to the next. I knew I was going to get rejected – it was undeniable, as much as I love my manuscript and everything about it, I understood sometimes it's just not for that specific agent. I received plenty of Dear writer/author rejections and it sort of stung, because I am basically assuming you didn't read it, but again I moved on. Sometimes, though, I didn't.

Another aspect to the dark side is the comparison, like I mentioned, but a different sort of comparison. Usually when someone rejects me, I just move on as mentioned above, but occasionally I would revisit the agency's website and get angry at the fact that they thought some Fabio cover, cheesy romance novel or some casual high school romance book with no unique story was better than mine. My reaction usually went two-fold. I either was happy the agency didn't pick me up because their taste is clearly not what I am looking for, or I would spiral into self-doubt over my abilities as a writer.

I had bad days. I had good days.

On a particularly good day I had gone to the nail salon and I got my first pair of acrylic nail tips in stiletto shape. For everybody who is confused by that expression – stiletto nails are like Adele nails – long, pointy, and almond shaped. Acrylic nails are fake nails created with liquid monomer and a powder polymer. Once it dries, it's virtually impossible to remove or even break without going back to the salon. If you do break them, it's basically like breaking your own nails right at the tip of your finger. Painful as fuck.

You want to know what's worse than having depression?

Having depression and anxiety at the same time while trying to pursue your passion.

The dark side of being an author besides the unwanted jealousy, unavoidable comparison, self-doubt in your work, and constant gripping fear of the future is the isolation.

I felt like nobody understood me. I was depressed because I missed my grandma, and I was anxious because I didn't know what my future looked like.

I'm well aware of how long the publishing journey is – I certainly don't expect people to know my characters or me over night. I just wanted a green light. The first step, and honestly, I just wanted to be happy. My sister and I always fight about whether it's better to know your passion and not have it realized or to not know your passion at all.

I argue that it's much worse to know your passion and not have it realized.

The depression helped expand the empty feeling in my chest with every single rejection I received, and my anxiety ripped my heart out every time I remembered what the rejection meant.

I had finally put myself first. I had finally found my calling in life. I had finally found a world I felt I belonged in, and it was rejecting me like a faulty heart transplant.

I was running in circles. Pushing. Going. I just couldn't understand why the world I would die for was killing me.

On a particularly bad day, I received five rejections within two hours.

That same day, I had a panic attack in the shower.

They say that when you have a panic attack you are supposed to look around and see five things, feel four things, hear three things, smell two things, and taste one thing. It's a grounding exercise, but having a panic attack is sort of like the beginning of a car accident. You know it's about to happen, there's nothing you can do to stop it, and the pain flows through you in slow motion.

The only thing I could touch were my acrylic nail. For a split second, they felt so heavy and I don't know why my reaction was to rip them off. I ripped my pinky nails off completely in the process but I didn't care. I felt nothing.

It's easy to say I was over reacting and sometimes I did feel like I was. After all, not everybody would like what I had written, and crying would not help. I convinced myself that maybe I was meant for something bigger, and that's why I hadn't been picked up yet. It was easy to believe that in the beginning, but the more rejections I received, the more doubtful I got.

I continued querying because I had inserted an idea in my brain somewhere, that if I didn't work extremely hard then I would not get what I wanted, and I didn't deserve it either. More recently I got into thinking back on my life as if to remember something bad I did. I convinced myself that I was being punished, but without sounding like an ego maniac, I never did anything with a malicious nature.

I got coffee for the people I worked without them asking for it, I drove distant friends to the airport, I took care of my parents, I held most of the burden during family issues, I never hurt anybody, I always tried to do the right thing, I gave up my childhood and the whole adulthood I have lived to make my parents proud, I always put other people first, I never got arrested, I never even got as much as a parking ticket, I held my depression and anxiety in as not to upset my parents.

I guess, it's what we are all taught – do the right thing and work hard, because if you do, you get what you deserve. I know life isn't fair, but this sucks.

I have put nothing but positive energy into the world and I feel like it has turned its back on me.

Remember that excel list of agents I have queried, I keep track of?

No, I am not going to release it like some sort of Watergate tape.

Do you want to take a guess as to what number I am up to?

380.

380 agents queried.

380 personalized emails.

380 attempts in one year.

2 Full Requests.

3 Partial Requests.

0 contracts signed.

Was this where you were expecting me to say – surprise! I actually got an agent while writing this piece. Yeah…you and I both. I actually got a rejection, but hey, that's nothing new.

I don't really know what to say. I wish this was a Hollywood ending, but I told you in the beginning no happy endings in this story. Yet.

Lesson of the Chapter

Find what you love to do and pursue it, even if it breaks
your heart.

EPILOGUE

11 Days Later

We made it guys and girls! I hope you are still reading....

Now, I was going to lie and tell you that I finished way before, but I promised honesty. It's Monday, which means it took me 11 days to finish, but I still think that's pretty fucking amazing. Writing close to 57,000 words in a under two weeks is something I am damn proud of.

So, my theory about the truth and how it's supposed to set you free. In a way, I guess it works. No, I don't have a deal set up or a contract on my desk, but that's not what I was hoping to get out of this.

Remember how I told you guys that my sister and I often argue about which is better – finding your passion and not having it realized or not knowing your passion at all?

My sister always argues that if you ask anybody who hasn't figured it out, they will absolutely say they would rather know their passion than walk around without a purpose, even if it means your passion is breaking your heart. Here's the thing about finding your passion.

Once you find it, nothing in the world will ever compare or be good enough for you.

If you haven't figured it out by now, I am a visual person.

I have a list taped on my wall. My desk is flushed against that same wall, so the list stares at me every single day. It's a visual reminder of what I want to accomplish in life.

1. #1 NYT Bestselling Author.

2. Own a home in California designed like my childhood home – in which I can enjoy and host my friends and family.

3. Explore the world.

4. Have a book tour and meet amazing people along the way.

5. Inspire young girls to create more art, use their voice, and make the world a better place.

6. Be a guest on The Late Show with Stephen Colbert.

7. Be happy.

It's not too much to ask for, and each thing has a reason behind it, even though my mom prefers I appear on Jimmy Fallon. As she puts it – "He seems like such a nice man."

Overall I just wanted to be an inspiration to people, I wanted them to know about my country, I felt responsible to get a message across, I didn't want people to feel as alone as I felt, I wanted to be the example I didn't have when I was younger, but maybe that was the problem.

I put too much pressure on my story. I put too much pressure on my characters. I wanted them to be what other people needed instead of what I needed. Everything felt so serious, like every single word I wrote had to mean something deeper.

In those motivational videos, I watch every once in a while, I came across a British philosopher, writer, and speaker, named Alan Watts, who mostly attempted to teach the culture of the East to the West. In a particular video, he said the following:

"No work or love will flourish out of guilt, fear, or hollowness of heart, just as no valid plans for the future can be made by those who have no capacity for living now."

Whether I like it or not, I wrote my young adult manuscript because I felt guilty, because I had a fear of the future, and because I felt hollow. I wanted to include every single aspect of my immigration story in ways that didn't make sense to my characters, instead of just letting it naturally flow out. I felt responsible for something.

Yes, I have edited my manuscript to just be a story I wanted to tell instead of focusing too deeply on the meaning of it all. I never write without purpose, so no matter how I tell that story, it will never lose meaning to me, and I am sure future readers.

So, did the truth set me free?

It did.

I have never had writer's block.

Knock on wood

I had a different type of block. I had the story of me. The collection of stories you just read, and I wrote them exactly how I remember them and with my genuine, honest voice – swearing and all. I feel relieved – like somehow now I am free. I am free to continue my manuscript however I think is best, and not because I am trying to include pieces of my personal story in there to make a point.

Make no mistake. There are pieces of me in every single character of that manuscript, and some of what they endure are things I have endured, but now they don't carry the burden of being anything else but what they are naturally meant to be.

They are meant to be a support system for those who need them.

Remember that. You create art – a form of expression – for those who need it, not those who criticize it.

I read an article once about Lil' Wayne. I know, I know. Just stay with me. He had a time when he was dealing with writer's block. It wasn't much of writer's block as it was way too many ideas in his head and on paper. He couldn't come up with a song because he wanted to include everything in one song. He wanted the song to tell all the thoughts in his head – which isn't possible. In a song, book, movie or any art form – it becomes a mess if you try and include all your thoughts in one piece and the message gets lost.

One day, he got in the studio and just started rapping. From all his notes, from the thoughts in his head – he emptied all that he was feeling on one track. He said everything he wanted to say. It ended up being a 35-minute rap called 10,000 bars.

From Albania, With Love

This collection of stories you just read is my 10,000 bars.

So, what now?

At the beginning of this journey, I didn't know if I would send this out to possibly be represented, but I have decided I will.

Why?

Fate – she keeps sending me signs like a bitch.

When I first started writing these stories at that awful job I had post grad, I made a list of topics I would potentially cover. You know – politically correct topics, what people wanted to hear – without all the swearing. That went out the fucking window. Anyway, because I am a neat freak I printed out a cover, and all the topics, and clipped them together. It's been sitting in a mail type organizer I have nailed to the wall next to my desk.

About two weeks ago, I printed out four little photos for Women's Day of the women who mean everything to me: my sister, my mom, my freshman year roommate – Thea, and my grandma. One of the photos was of my mom and my grandma on my mom's wedding day. I clipped the photos to my mailing organizer – on the same shelf as my printed-out first and extremely different version of what this piece became.

I don't have much on my desk right now – I don't like clutter, but I have these three little stones Thea mailed to me with my birthday present. She decorated them with some gold markers and wrote a word on each; create, dream, and love.

I would be lying to you if I said I wasn't thinking about if I was going to pursue this after I was done while I was writing it, but right in the middle of writing chapter ten, the photo of my grandma and my mom on her wedding day fell about two feet from the industrial binder clip that was holding it and fell on top of the three stones sitting on my desk.

I know what you're thinking.

Really, though? Are you fucking serious? It was just the wind.

I would have said the same, but my window wasn't open and I was sitting down, AND, it was stuffed in between the other photos.

I don't know, maybe it's irrational, but I will remind you that I was the girl who thought seeing a crow was a sign that I was going to die. It won't hurt if I actually believed in a positive sign.

What do I have to lose? The worse that can happen is I get rejected and we all know that's not a problem for me.

Well, that's it guys!

Maybe you learned something, maybe you didn't. Maybe you care, maybe you don't. It's alright either way, because…. you guessed it – this is my story.

Are those all the stories I have to tell? Nope.

Was I 100% honest with you? Yep.

From Albania, With Love

Will there be a follow up? Probably not; my made-up world and characters await me, and I miss those bastards terribly.

If you were allegedly mentioned in these stories – Congrats!

If you didn't like how you were portrayed – I don't give a fuck.

If you thought you were going to be in these stories, but weren't – clearly your presence was not that special in my world or maybe you are just part of the stories I haven't told yet.

Take your pick.

So, what now?

According to the steps of getting published, I should edit, but will I?

Nope. I will check for grammar mistakes, because I told you – I am awful at following grammar rules. Everything else will remain the same, because this was an honest piece, and it will remain that. How can you believe me?

You can't, but I didn't lie this whole time, why would I start now?

So, what comes next?

I have one last theory, though. Actually, more of an experiment.

As you saw I have had plenty of signs that I was supposed to be a writer and tell my story – a story I am going to assume is this one, to begin my journey. All my life I have been told, if something is meant to be for you, it will be, just as long as your heart is pure. I am not going to get any purer than right now. This piece was like 95% pure cut cocaine – I swear I don't do drugs. Just hear me out.

It took me 25 years to be honest with myself and finally tell the story that came first, so in that spirit, and since this is truly when my journey is beginning, I will pick 25 agents to query. I have a pretty extensive and detailed excel list to choose from, so it should not be a problem.

25 agents who represent young adult as well as non-fiction, because we all know fiction is my reason to be on this earth. I will query these 25 agents only and if I get bite back, then I guess this was really the story I was supposed to tell first. If I don't get a bite back, I don't really know what the plan is, but I hope I don't find out.

Ugh... now I have to go write a new query letter. Fuck.

I told you guys about my fears, my life, and a lot more along the way, but here's a last piece of honesty from me.

My biggest fear was always telling this real and personal story. I hid behind my desire to help others, behind my fiction writing, behind doubt, behind depression, behind fear of being labeled different and weird, behind my past, and I especially hid behind the self I portrayed to the world.

I wish this could be a Hollywood type happy ending, but I am glad you came on this journey with me because I finally realize who I am meant to be.

With that, and with love, I leave you with a last lesson.

Lesson of the Journey

No matter your past, you always choose who you want to become. Don't ever let anybody else make that decision for you.

Migena Dulaj

AN EPILOGUE OF AN EPILOGUE
131 Days Later

I'm back, bitches!!

I'm joking, honestly – thanks for buying this & for reading this far. You're a phenomenal human being.

You are probably wondering why you are reading an epilogue of an epilogue. At the beginning of this journey/diary I promised you honesty in all forms of my life, including this piece, so once again I will not lie to you.

If you are reading this it means that I did not get an agent for this particular memoir/diary/real life story – whatever you want to call it. Actually, it means that I am not signed with an agent at all. Let's get down to what happened these past four months.

I edited – grammar only – then I wrote a query letter. Fucking hate those. Anyways, I picked from the list of agents I had, and even found some new ones, but I always made sure that they represented both genres (non-fiction and young adult). My whole 25 queries bullshit I told you about last chapter quickly went out the fucking window, because you guessed it – I don't take my own advice. I convinced myself that that was a stupid idea, and that I needed to work hard to get this published, so I sent a total of 56 queries for this manuscript.

From Albania, With Love

Oh, and by the way, when pitching a non-fiction, you often have to write a proposal, because typically you haven't written the manuscript yet – it's just an idea.

Well, my idea was done, written, edited, and ready to meet the world.

Honestly, I thought it was fucking exhausting and ridiculous to have to write a proposal for something already completed, but I did, and I'm glad I did. You see, in a proposal you usually have to include target audience, possible marketing tools, etc.

I told you I don't like math and that is still very valid, however, this was the one-time numbers were my friends. There are 3.7 million Albanian immigrants in Europe, estimated 180,000 Albanians in the US (there might be more, we don't really fill out the census), 37 million second generation immigrants in the United States, and 244 million persons living in a country they were not born in. In short, us immigrants, are every fucking where, and we make the world a better place to live in, but what this really told me is that there is a market for my book. I didn't need the numbers to convince myself – I saw it among young people, people my age when I was in college, I saw it on social media, on TV shows and movies, and every avenue possible. I knew people could relate to this manuscript, because it's exactly what I wish I had when I was doubting myself, who I was, if my background made me who I am, what I wanted my life to look like, and especially when I felt like the whole world was against me.

It wasn't only the numbers though – it was the facts. The facts I had to deal with as a woman. If you read this whole book then you know what I am talking about, but really, go on Google and type Albanian authors.

I'll save you a trip. Here are the stats.

52 Authors (Including Enver Hoxha – *yeah, what the actual fuck*)

8 are women. All who live in Europe/Albania. 6 are poets. 1 journalist. 1 screenplay writer.

Zero novelists that I know of. Zero Albanian born US citizens. Zero talking about the immigrant experience, educating the world on Albania, or breaking barriers/stereotypes in the US. The most important fact for me, was that there was no prominent Albanian female figure in the literary world in the US showing young Albanian girls in the US and in Albania that you can do anything in the world – there was nobody they could see themselves in or find hope in. As depressing as this fact is, I thought it brought on a wonderful and unique opportunity.

Well, apparently, most agents think that only celebrities or experts should write memoirs, and to a certain degree I understand what they mean, and it's not their fault. Blame society. Blame publishing companies. Blame popularity. Blame social norms. Blame whoever and whatever you want, but it won't make a difference. Blaming others for the lack of the sort of life you wish you had will not only make you miserable, but it will also never help materialize your dreams into reality.

From Albania, With Love

Here's the truth I should have realized, but was hiding from. This piece of non-fiction work, this memoir, this collection of stories was never meant to fit into a standard box. I should have known since the beginning. My young adult manuscript didn't feel like it belonged anywhere either, just like me. It is near/distant future with uniquely set up governments, but it isn't dystopian. It has royalty and competitions, but it's not fantasy. It has future technological advances, but it's not science fiction. It has epic love connections and dramatic elements, but it isn't a romance. All in all, it simply does not fit into a box. My other manuscript aside, this manuscript you are reading was meant to be shared. It was not meant to become a long-winded project, it was natural – just like the way I wrote it.

So, what was stopping me?

I consider myself extremely lucky to live in a country, and a time that allows me to instantly share my story with the whole world, but I was stuck – frozen in my expectations.

Expectations will destroy your life.

You see, no matter if they have ever admitted it or not, writers who want to become published, have this expectation. You write a book, you send queries, you struggle, you get a big shot New York agent, you get a publishing deal, you get a movie deal, and on and on. It's not our fault – we see it everywhere. In movies, on social media, on the news. So, we grow to unknowingly expect this path to publishing for ourselves too, because it's the normal thing, and when it doesn't happen that way, or at all, we see failure in ourselves, which is fucked up, because writers are the most amazing artists.

Here's the thing, the moment you realize those expectations of success and a *"certain path"* were set by someone just like you, another person, you free yourself. You can now make your own path into whatever life you deem successful, by your own rules.

I think you know by now that I seldom take my own advice, so it took me a really long time to get here, but the only thing I never lost while querying this specific work, is the belief that people need this collection of stories. No matter how many times agents told me the market is saturated, a memoir should be written by a celebrity, or just straight up didn't answer, there was something in my bones telling me that they were wrong, telling me that this needs to be out in the world, but my immigrant child syndrome resurfaced.

You see, I was expecting my path to go the right way, a certain way, so that I could make my parents proud, my country proud, and conform into a social norm of success. Self-publishing is not typically associated with success, so I never even considered it – I actually thought it was fucking insane, but here's something to remember.

While, yes, sending out your work to be represented is a huge leap, and scary – self-publishing is having the most blinding faith in your work and yourself. It's fucking terrifying. You have to believe without anybody else's approval or support that your work deserves to be out in the world, and have a shot at possibly changing someone's life for the better.

From Albania, With Love

You would think that I would know by now that I'm not normal – in the nicest way possible. The very first thing you read about me was that I split my head open to fit in, and realized that fitting in is bad for your health, but I didn't take that piece of information when I ventured into the publishing world. I went the traditional route, when we all know nothing about my life or path into writing has been traditional, so maybe I just need to make my own path.

If they don't believe, maybe I have to show them.

Now, I promised not to lie, so here's the truth;

I would love to be with a publishing company, with a supportive and understanding agent. I would love to be a New York Times Best Seller, I would love to hold my book in my hands, but none of those things would ever mean as much to me as my work changing someone's life. If those things can happen together, then great, but for now I'm just going to be unapologetically myself, and focus on getting my story out to the people I have faith need it. I'm a mess of emotions just knowing that my work will be out in the world soon.

What now?

Some of you might be asking if I will still pursue my young adult novel.

Answer: Hell, to the fucking yeah.

I never stopped believing in those characters, and while it may seem crazy to some people, they helped me finally believe in myself, my art, my work, and my message to the world.

I talked to you about passion before, and I meant what I said – you have to want something as bad as you want to breathe.

I love my work, my characters, and the worlds I have built more than life its self, so no, I will never stop pushing, writing, working, editing, creating, and most importantly believing in myself. I have simply reached a point in which I am tired of waiting for someone else to believe in my dream, I am tired of expecting a select group of people to understand me or my work, I am tired of constantly looking for approval in a soul crushing industry, and I'm especially exhausted from the endless waiting when I know I could do something myself. I'm done waiting for the miracle, the hail Mary, the light at the end of the tunnel, and I am lighting that bitch up myself.

455.

That's the final query count. That's the final rejection count.

I know some of you are like, damn, *that's fucked up*, and it is, but know this – I'll *NEVER* quit, even if that number gets to 1,000, but for now I'm going a different route.

A new route.

I'm not the first or last one to go down a different publishing road. I'm not the only one with a story to tell. I'm certainly not the only immigrant in the United States or the only Albanian. I'm not the only writer out there.

But I had something to share, and now that I have, I feel remarkably free.

From Albania, With Love

I saw a post from Sophia Bush on Instagram the other day. It was a poem from the great Audre Lorde – writer, feminist, and civil rights activist, and it said the following.

"I want to live the rest of my life, however long or short, with as much sweetness as I can decently manage, loving all the people I love, and doing as much as I can of the work I still have to do. I am going to write fire until it comes out of my ears, my eyes, my nose holes, - everywhere, until it's every breath I breathe. I am going to go out like a fucking meteor."

That's how I feel at this specific moment – free, passionate, inspired, excited, and ready. I want to live my life like this until I have done everything I need to do, and live every moment I am meant to live. This time, I will take my own advice and step into this unclear path with undying and blinding belief in myself.

I truly hope you have found something in this collection of stories to inspire you, to make you feel understood, to grant you peace, or to grant you hope.

I will leave you with one last lesson.

Final Lesson

You can never change the world if you fit into a mold
others have created as their normal.

ACKNOWLEDGEMENTS

I was expecting to write these thank yous in a completely different scenario – like first young adult novel type of acknowledgements that I had thought and thought about over these past three years. You know, thanking editors, agents, publishing houses, and such, but I do believe being thankful and humble is not only necessary, but extremely important to have a pure heart and a happy life. I know by the time I get to writing the acknowledgements for my young adult manuscript many things will have changed. I will more than likely have many more people to thank and a much fuller heart, but for now, here it is.

Mom, you are the most phenomenal woman I have ever known. You taught me perseverance, strength, and kindness on a level I never knew possible. I will forever be in awe of the way you always give people the benefit of the doubt, and always see the best in everybody. If it wasn't for your undying love and belief in me, I don't know that anybody would be reading this or any future work from me. You are my rock, my warrior, and my heart. I love you into infinity and beyond any limit.

Dad, thank you for never allowing my Albanian heritage and pride to die or fade, as much as I was resistant to it, as much as I wanted to belong elsewhere, you always made sure to talk about Albania, the news, our history and many other things I probably didn't want to hear at the time.

Chewbacca (Nope, not the one y'all are thinking about), you are my ride or die in this whole process. From the first moment I decided to write, you were the one who yelled at me to stop fiercely editing the first chapter. Instead, you forced me to have a chapter ready for you when you got home from work. If it wasn't for that I wouldn't have a 110,000-word YA manuscript that I am extremely proud of, and I am forever grateful for that. You have been my partner in crime and #1 supporter, not only in this writing journey, but also in the journey of life. I love you to pieces.

Grandma & Grandpa Çaçi, I know you aren't technically in this world anymore, but you never left my heart. Grandpa, thank you for showing me how a real man is supposed to treat women, and especially what unconditional love looks like, and feels like. Grandma, thank you for your humor through tough times, your feminism in a time of inequality, your show of resistance against the norm, your positive attitude even when things couldn't get worse, your love when I felt like I wasn't enough, and your guidance – even now. I'm sorry I didn't tell you I loved you nearly as much as I should have, but just like I know you're guiding me, you know what having you in my life has meant to me.

Jillian & the Friot Family. Chris & Janet, thank you for being the best surprise of my life, the kindest and sincerest family I have ever met, and especially for raising the most amazing daughter I have the privilege of calling my friend. Jillian, you are amazing, sweet, and incredible – I could continue to list the best adjectives I can think of, but just know this, you have been a beacon of light in my life since we met, and you have become my family. I don't think I could ever find the words to tell you how much your true and genuine support has meant to me over the years.

Carly, you have been my sounding board since high school, and one of the only lasting friendships from that time in my life. Thank you for being a geek with me and sending hand written letters to each other when we were in college, for always encouraging the artist in me to surface, for listening to me, and for supporting me without a hint of judgement – no matter what crazy ideas I had.

Jenna, thank you for the coffee dates, for hearing me bitch about any and everything, for introducing Fiona into my life, and for the random, but ever therapeutic car rides to get tea.

Daniela, you were my first reader, my only reader, of everything I've done. I was met with nothing but excitement when I told you I was in the process of writing a book. Thank you for being you, for listening to my ranting, for dealing with me when I become extremely anti-social, for understanding me distancing away from the whole world when writing or editing, and for sometimes forcing me to live my life in the present.

Mr. James Lee, while this is not a work of fiction, it was my fictional work which got me here, to this point. It was your class, your passion for teaching, for English, for being creative, and for lifting up stories by immigrants since way back in the day, that kick started my interest in writing fiction, and I sincerely thank you.

Professor Mary Lyons, thank you for encouraging me to tell my story, even if at the time, I thought the idea was completely insane. It was the seed you planted in my mind about my background, and a potential career as a writer that began this long journey. Thank you for seeing in my writing, what I now see too.

Monique, you held it down since the very beginning – when I was a scared freshman who didn't have a room key. The late-night shopping runs, the coffee breaks in your office, the long dinners discussing topics close to our heart – these are happy memories I'm eternally appreciative to have. I will be forever grateful for your continued friendship and support.

Albania, it may not have seemed like it a few times, but I do love you, and everything I have become due to you. I'm thrilled that I told a few of your stories, and hopefully people will have a chance to see your beauty, grace, and strength. I can't wait to come home.

Immigrants near and far, don't be afraid to show your culture – it makes you who you are, it makes you unique, and it makes you a beautiful human being, no matter what anybody with hate in their heart says about you. Our diversity is celebrated, our strength is astounding, our perseverance is to be revered, and our open and accepting hearts are an example for all. Never forget that, and never ever forget that there will always be more light than darkness in the world – just make sure to lift up those who shine bright, not those who reflect darkness.

Ladies of all shapes, sizes, colors, backgrounds, and sexualities, I love and respect you all very much. We are all phenomenal beings, and the closest thing to real life magic. We can do any and everything when we embrace our differences, lift each other up during our times of need, and celebrate each other in successes.

Stephen Colbert, my TV husband and overall talented human being, thank you for getting me through that awful job I had a few months out of college. I was miserable and bored, so I would watch clips of the Colbert Show, under my desk, to keep myself laughing and happy. Thank you for being a shining example in a dark time. I'll meet you soon enough – when I appear on your show (*fingers crossed*)

Anthony, barista extraordinaire at the Starbucks I go to at least twice a day. You're the real OG – you always got my drink order right, and you didn't say anything that one time I'm pretty sure you noticed I was crying as I rolled through the drive through. It was a rough day, but I appreciate you just handing me my usual and pretending like everything was cool.

Last, but certainly far from least, **my readers**. I don't know where to begin. I don't know how many of you are really even going to buy this book, but here's the thing, even if it's just one person who buys it, and it helps you in some way, I've achieved my goal. If you are reading this and you are going through a rough time, believe me – it will get better. If you really need someone to talk to, just email me. If you are reading this, and you feel like giving up on your dreams, take it from someone who has been there, don't do it. It will break your heart into a thousand pieces the way a rejection never could. If you are reading this, and you are thinking about starting a new hobby, taking a new career path, pursuing a dream, or beginning a new journey of any sort, and are unsure if it's the right thing for you, but it makes you happy, take this as a sign from the universe that you should do it.

I said this before, but thank you, thank you, thank you, from the very depths of my soul, for purchasing this book, and taking the time to read it. It's funny, as a writer I can probably describe a scenario or person a million different ways, but I don't think I'll ever be able to capture or express to you what emotions are flowing through my veins right now, as I imagine someone reading this very sentence.

Never forget that you are loved, you are needed, and you are very important to this world.

I love you all.

With Love,
Migena

THANK

YOU

Follow Migena
for book updates, a glimpse into her journey, photos of
books, food, coffee (cups and cups of coffee), and
everything in between.

Facebook.com/MigenaDulajAuthor
Instagram.com/MigenaDulaj
Pinterest.com/MigenaDulaj
MigenaDulaj.tumblr.com
Twitter.com/MigenaDulaj

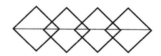

Subscribe for Migena's Newsletter
for giveaways, books news, and monthly ramblings
about any and everything.

www.migenadulaj.com

CPSIA information can be obtained
at www.ICGtesting.com
Printed in the USA
BVOW09s1917191017
498047BV00008B/189/P